Art versus beauty

ART *versus* BEAUTY

When stones dance with eggs

ADRIAN DAVID

LUDION

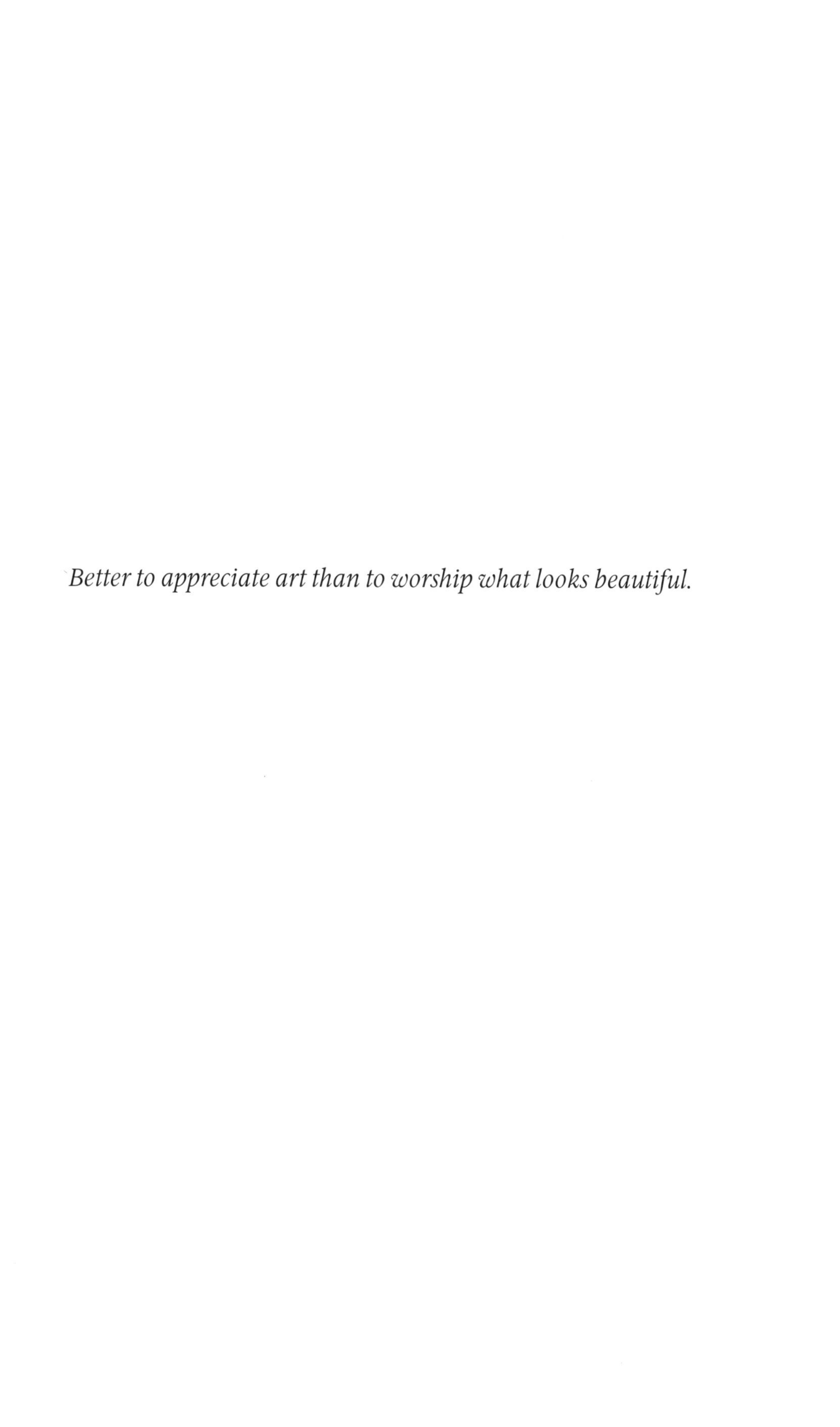

Better to appreciate art than to worship what looks beautiful.

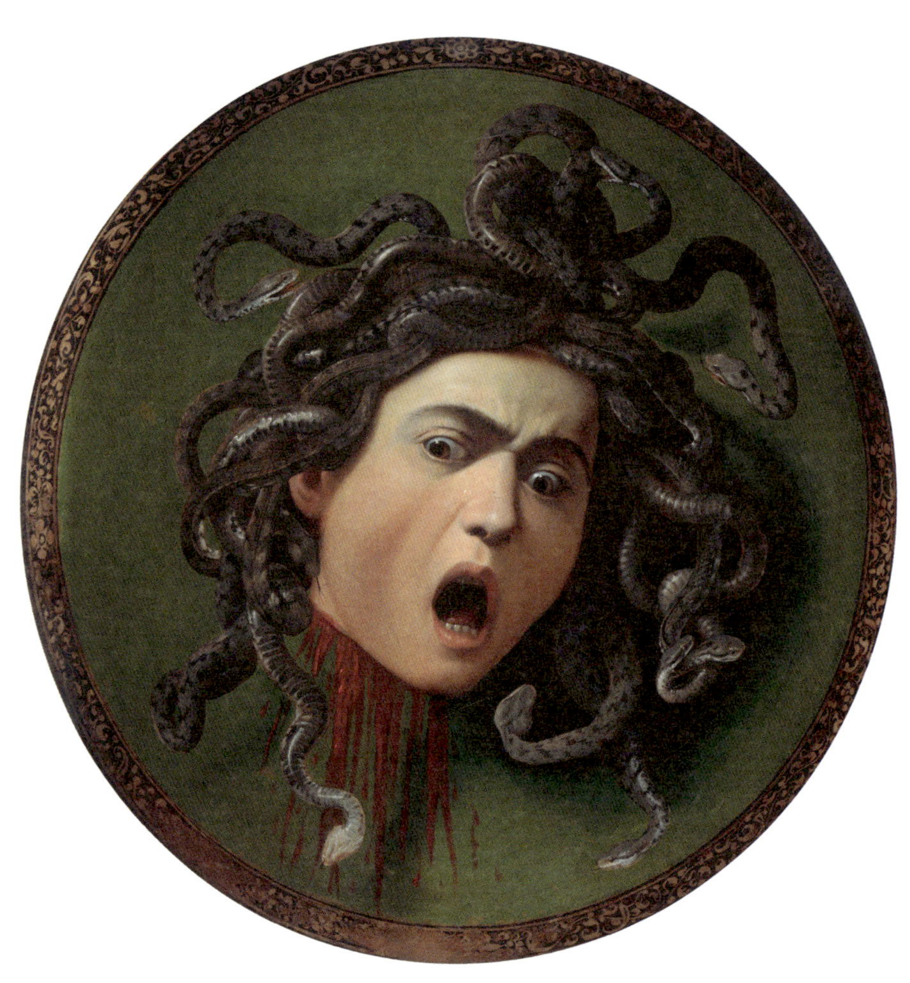

Michelangelo Merisi da Caravaggio
Medusa, 1595–98
Oil on canvas, mounted on wood, 60 × 55 cm
Florence, Le Gallerie degli Uffizi

PROLOGUE

The mythological figure of Medusa has inspired a great many artists. And not just because of her monstrous appearance: there was much more to it than that. She is a fascinating but simultaneously tragic figure. A fact that calls for a little explanation.

Medusa was exceptionally beautiful at first, but she lived in a place where the sun never shone and the girl yearned for different climes. Athena, the greatest goddess of the pantheon, begrudged Medusa the sun, preferring to keep her beauty hidden away in darkness. One day, burning with passion, Medusa made love to Poseidon in the very temple of Athena. The divine virgin sought her revenge by transforming the transgressor's gorgeous locks into a nest of writhing snakes. Now Medusa became the terror of all those who were drawn to her beauty: anyone who gazed on her lovely face was instantly and irrevocably turned to stone.

Medusa and Athena each have their special significance in art history: the former is frequently depicted as a terrifying beauty with serpents for hair, while the latter was adopted as the divine protector of artists. Their shared myth is a perfect analogy for how the urge for beauty has become fossilized in art too.

DESTRUCTIVE TOLERANCE

Anyone who pays attention to art knows that when you see something new, something previously unknown, a special effort is needed to understand it. Consequently, the world of art has always been a quarrelsome alliance, incapable of shying away from the slightest opportunity for an argument. Those brave enough to create something new and those who seek to judge it need to be open to this fact. Contemporary art sometimes provokes the response 'I could have done that myself'. But anyone who makes such a claim is naive about art if not entirely out of touch with it. Commenting negatively on the unfamiliar implies a lack of knowledge and study – precisely the things you need when addressing anything new. Meanwhile, a great many successive new styles have developed throughout the ages. Taking art in its entirety, neither the technical ability of those who call themselves artists, nor the amount of time they spend on a work, has any real value. Defining art based purely on formal characteristics is the wrong place to start. We need to set aside preconceived ideas about what art is. Better to recognize the pattern of evolution in each period and be guided by it.

Art is a growth that feeds above all on restlessness, making it capable of devouring an entire life. It will passionately charm you and never leave your life undisturbed again. If you prefer a quiet and peaceful existence, you are best advised to live without art. Artists, patrons, historians and a whole lot of art lovers know that living for art can become a fanatical addiction. What art requires, in other words, are the kind of enthusiasts who are willing to train their brains and who sense the presence of art like some life-affirming angel. Attentive observers like this live symbiotically with a higher power, which will take the works of art they judge to be good and steer them through the times to come. So it is not unusual for the public at large to accept the patron's opinion only decades after a work was created. There is no objective truth about a work of art and 'art' itself is impossible to define conclusively. An artistic judgement based on scholarly analysis can never substitute for a personal judgement.

A work of art is not trapped in the particularity of its creator's world, but keeps generating new messages; to such an extent that a successful work is sufficiently rich in interpretations that it can even appeal to audiences from other cultures. It is an innocent luxury: it can hardly be called indispensable to our existence, yet it enhances and satisfies our seeing. Art offers its viewers a freedom in which they can use their own interpretative capacity to sense an involvement. A universal work of art that writes history places itself beyond the circumstances of its own production and is able in turn to break free from further constraints. It is a work that will ultimately tell us something about our world; it embodies a vision of how human beings are, or have become. Art is much broader than the particular experience of the artist, making it the most indefinable phenomenon of all and one that casts doubt on any attempt at definition. Anyone who wishes to experience art with genuine value will thus have to think about it. Art is inseparable from philosophical reflection and philosophy is the seedbed for understanding real art.

Many would argue that the most important facet of art is imagination. The dominant position afforded to this can, however, sidetrack viewers and lead them astray. Imagination, aesthetics and beauty might be central to any discussion about art, but they ought not to be considered as absolute values. Untrammelled fantasy does not add value to a work of art: if anything, excess is a constraint. Does an excessive artwork still have room for a civilizing message? Bombast obliterates any scope for understanding the essence of art, which is rarely a good thing. It is always necessary to criticize anything viewed too quickly as art. Creating art is more about restraint and the intellectual involvement that keeps everything under control. This is where the major difference is found between professional and occasional artists, and it is here too that the idea of 'I could do that too' perishes.

Art lovers have been served up a wide range of creations in recent decades, persuading them that they are duty-bound to admire every artistic form that continues to arrive en masse. Yet nothing could be further from the truth. Even those who have feelings about what they see must still ask themselves precisely what it is they are feeling. The answer has to be more than simply the pleasure of being seduced by an abundance of imagination.

What if the excess of today's art has diminished our concentration on what ought to be seen? If the plethora of art on offer has resulted in a loss of density and that the focus required to understand it is invariably destroyed? This superabundance reduces every exhibition of contemporary art to a procession that immunizes the passionate visitor against any possibility of a critical approach. So many images are wrongly held out as 'art' nowadays that the necessary understanding of the word is steadily losing its critical aspect.

The number of people who dutifully contemplate this excess is growing all the time. A bigger population with more leisure time amplifies the urge for experiences of any kind. There is nothing inherently worrisome about a zeitgeist packed with abundance. However, the sheer number of works that are seen and are considered as art points towards a more alarming situation. It is not the human imagination that needs to be resisted within the growth of a culture: on the contrary, we see it as a gift. All the same, we need to understand that in times of excess it is up to art lovers themselves to build their resistance and to adopt a more critical stance towards what they are being served up. Viewing every object that pertains to art in one way or another results in a corrosive tolerance. If you accept everything that is offered to you, you risk blinding yourself. And if the immense tolerance of this group helps stimulate such excess, the result will be an inexorable mishmash of everything that huddles together under the banner of 'art'. When much-loved art lulls viewers into a sweet slumber, it is hard to distinguish the living from the dead any more among the admiring public. If the most societally adored and readily selling artificial artist creates solely for admirers who yearn for familiar flavours, art becomes utopian. Creators exist to serve viewers with their pre-digested recipe, their imagination and their forms, all produced within the old style and technique, which everyone ideally can understand. The apathetic acceptance of every kind of art exhibition equates to a mass event that infinitely multiplies the whole agglomeration of uncritically accepted creations.

What is already known lacks any militant desire and in reality has nothing to say to us as contemporary work within the evolution of our time. It panders to a public that steers clear of any intellectual effort and, with its lack of artistic insight, also tends to mock real innovators. Focused on their own self-protection, these apathetic spectators are afraid of friction and disorder in their back yard. They would rather hide away behind the old ingredients of art. Not much new is going into art today. There is an unbridled receptiveness that needs to be broken through and a creative excess that must be eliminated as quickly as possible. There is a need for substantial resistance. There is no element of historical knowledge in public receptivity to art, which means we must ensure that art lovers do not lose their self-critical faculties. Rather than giving art a huge amount of space, it should have that space reduced to help preserve genuine artistic creativity.

Anyone who has studied art and considered it across the entirety of its history knows that it is impossible to define the concept of 'beauty'. Experience, reflection, consideration and even meditative approaches, by contrast, continue to allow us to explore the labyrinth of art. You can immerse yourself in art or lose yourself in it. Art lovers do not get lost, they immerse themselves. They love creation provided that time maintains the evolution of art as a necessity. Art needs to respond to the demands of its time and we must remain receptive to that.

BEAUTY AS MISCONCEPTION

The public expects to find its own, self-conceived standards of beauty in everything it considers to be art. It believes it can find a characteristic in art that defines it as such, an aspect so recognizable that it causes that same public to find the work of art 'beautiful'. But what is this aspect of art which means that every work that has become famous falls under the common descriptor of 'beautiful'? What exactly are the conditions for deeming a creation aesthetic, for defining it as beautiful? What received quality of beauty connects the virtuosity of Pieter Paul Rubens' naturalistic depictions with the garish colours of James Ensor's triumphant *Christ's Entry into Brussels*? What beauty is shared by René Magritte's nude *Magie noire* and the de-eroticized, chaotic nudes of Francis Bacon? How can we link the beauty of Frans Hals' seventeenth-century portraits with the photo paintings of Gerhard Richter? Do any properly reasoned definitions exist that would allow all these things to be substantively deemed 'beautiful'? Anyone who seeks beauty in art needs to ask themselves 'why?'

'Beautiful' is the most common description for anything that makes us feel good. Its application comes from the contemplation of particular forms that are engaging, satisfying and exalting. The feeling offered by this beauty is an entirely sensory experience, it is abstract and it concerns only what we see, nothing more. It moulds looking into a single word and robs the object of any purpose behind its existence. The supposedly 'beautiful', as an answer to the above questions, is utterly meaningless here. 'Beautiful' cannot be defined. It is a subjective judgement of taste that does not tell us anything about what is being viewed. Any object deemed to be beautiful without any further intellectual interpretation by its creator receives nothing more than a worthless label, which is secondary to the significance of the object itself. If aesthetic beauty is bound up unconditionally with the reality principle, there is a major communication breakdown with the world of art. The perception of beauty is a highly unstable sensation.

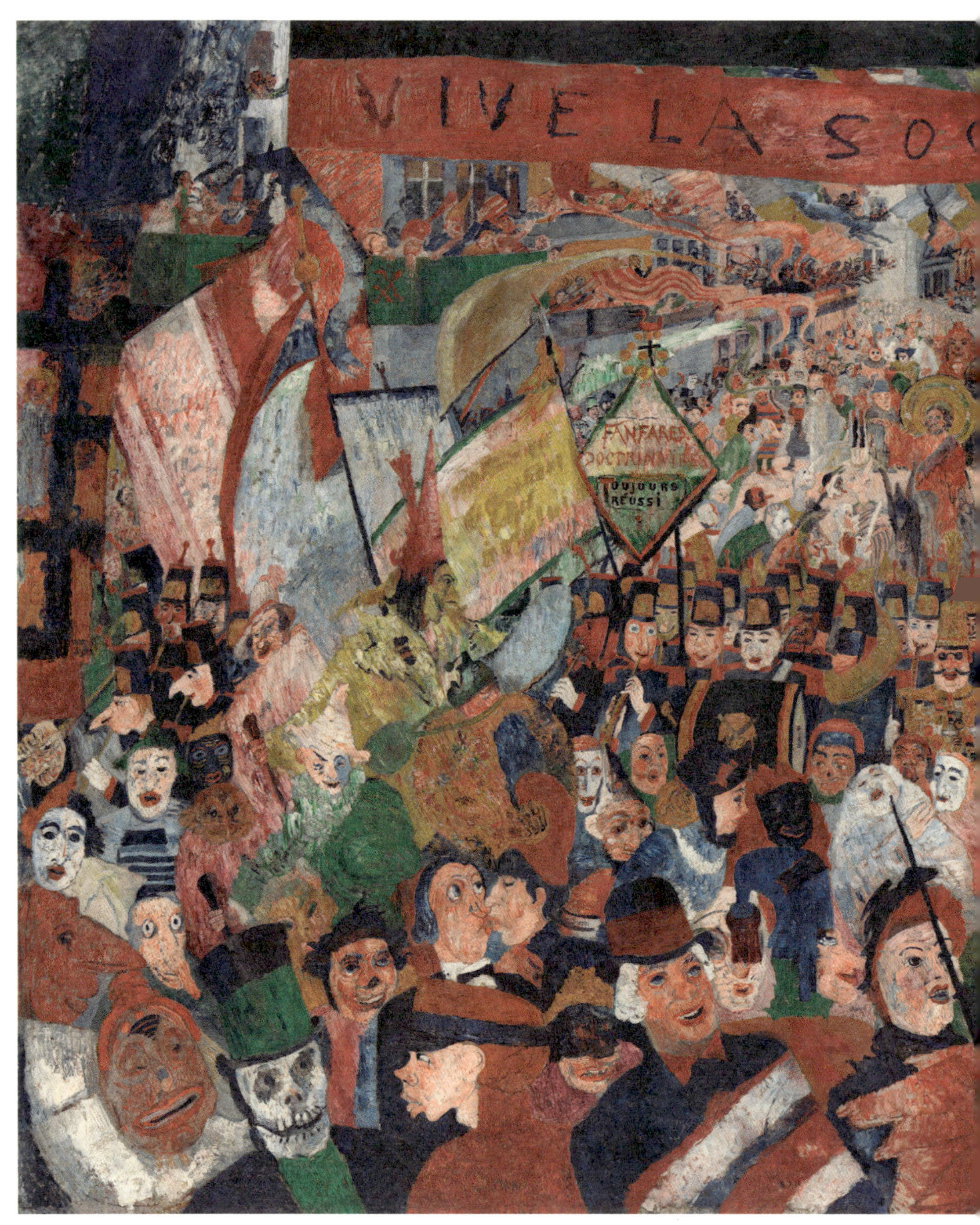

James Ensor
Christ's Entry into Brussels in 1889, 1888
Oil on canvas, 253 × 431 cm
Los Angeles, Getty

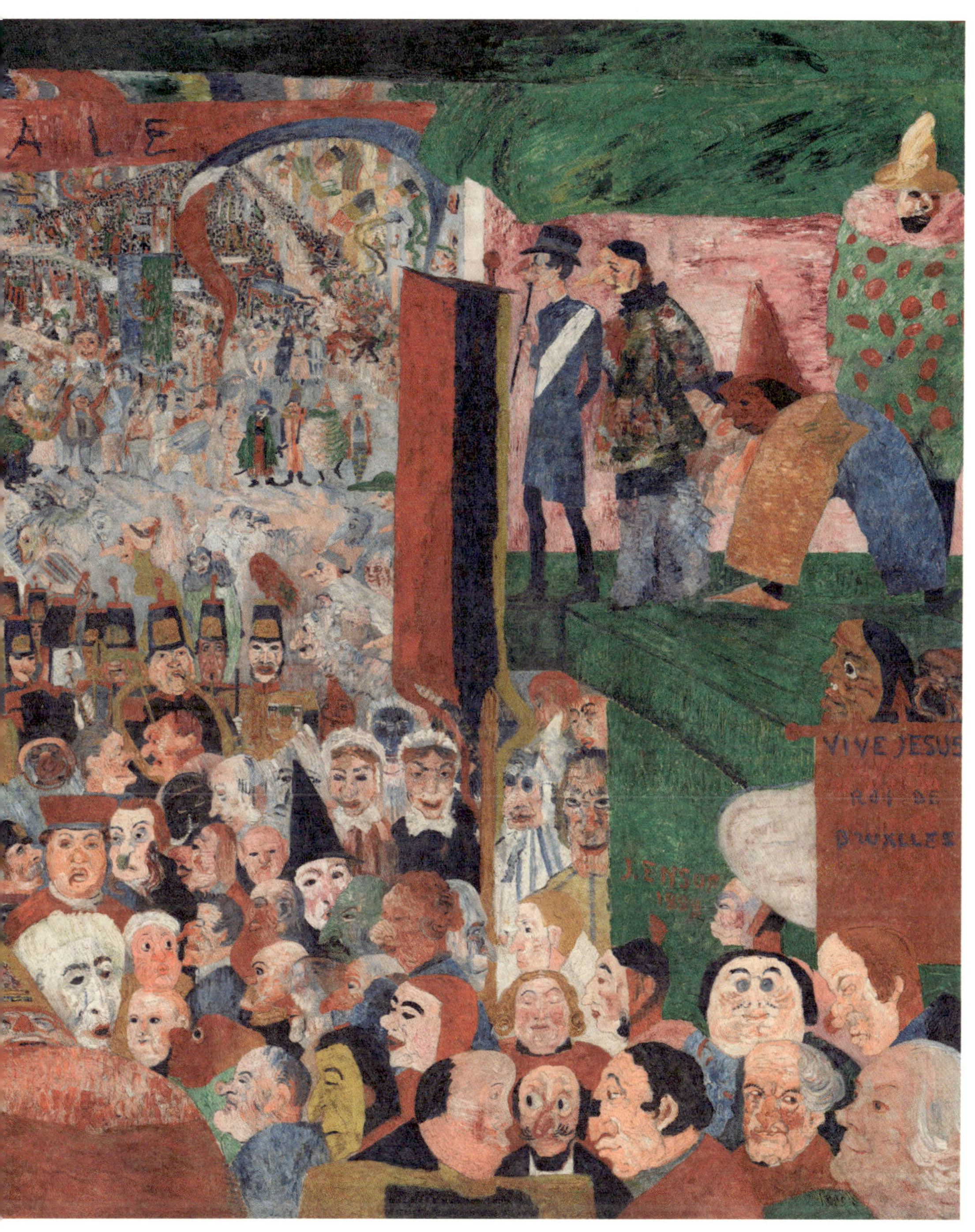
ALE
VIVE JESUS
ROI DE
BRUXELLES
J. ENSOR

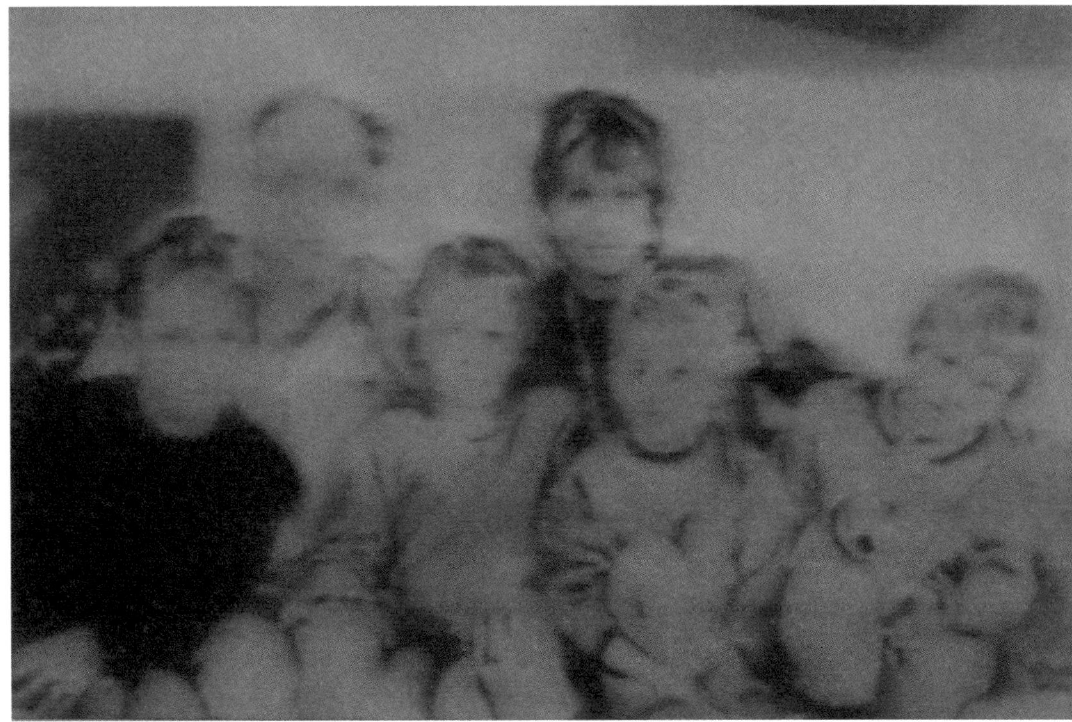

The German philosopher Immanuel Kant raised art to a higher, universal moral level in the eighteenth century. He understood how art had evolved over the centuries and now that it had taken on a freer form, he was in a better position to tackle the concept of 'beauty'. Kant took the view that beauty could be judged as a symbol of universal morality. This implies a necessity for more than the formation of an image, given that the sense of beauty also requires a degree of mental effort. Consequently, the beauty of universal taste has to be brought to life primarily via a process of thought. According to Kant, a good work of art connects with the mind, stimulates our thinking and offers us a more meaningful life. The existence of art is hence considered a motivating force by which to give more meaning to our own lives.

It is important to realize that aesthetic beauty is not therefore a property of an object as such, and that a painting with immediate appeal does not derive any added value as a result. A work cannot be considered beautiful merely for the material from which it is made, nor by what it represents. A judgement of beauty that elicits pleasure and engages with the physical aspects of the beheld object is not a legitimate art judgement. A work of art can only become important by virtue of the fact that

Gerhard Richter
Ruhnau Family, 1969
Oil on canvas, 130 × 200 cm
San Francisco Museum of Modern Art

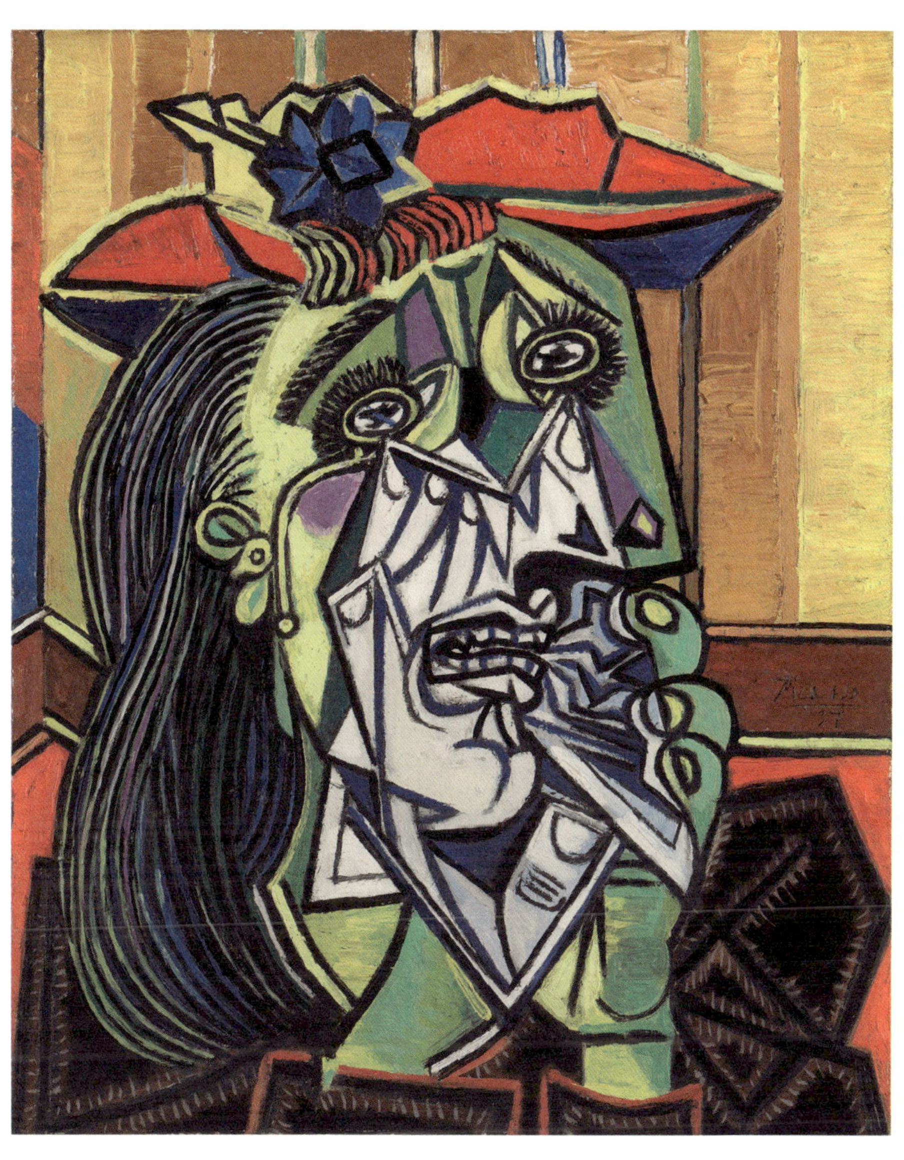

Pablo Picasso
Weeping Woman, 1937
Oil on canvas, 60 × 50 cm
London, Tate Modern

you can think about it. It is here that you find the gateway into art. If the beautiful painting is given the freedom to exist as it is and nothing more than what it is, we arrive at the paradox of Kant's 'purposiveness without purpose' (*Zweckmäßigkeit ohne Zweck*). What the philosopher clearly demonstrated with his critical logic is that the 'taste judgement' – or, on an aesthetic level, the 'beauty judgement' – might amount to the highest freedom, but it also entails every form of meaninglessness with the least responsibility. Those who prefer to focus on the grandeur behind art know that famous artists in every era have had a broad knowledge, possessed literary capacities and, in addition to a lot of humour, also had the common sense to deliver their message. These great artists thought clearly and so were very much not the authors of brainless creations: they were universal artists who created new forms through their self-exploration. They brought a new style, which imposed itself, and with which the art-hungry enthusiast gladly entered into an intellectual confrontation.

The emergence of modern art caused a scandal, but at the same time it strongly influenced the evolution of art. For many observers, the *antimodel* or defiguration of twentieth-century art made a mockery of realistic painting: innovators were branded as incompetents and pilloried accordingly. Even before he embarked on Cubism, Pablo Picasso (1881–1973), one of the founders of modern art, had a message to convey in works that were nonetheless naturalistic and figurative. Nowhere in his art is there any trace of childish clumsiness or naivety. There are no drawings by the young Picasso in which his talent might have been noticed at an early stage. Many children's drawings are quickly deemed to show talent, but the young masters who made them disappear just as quickly. Artists have to start all over again and rid themselves of any previous, childish vision. A true artist goes much further – away from the innocent, spontaneous creations of the child's hand, and beyond the subsequent meticulousness and precision of academic skills. Pablo's father was a drawing teacher while Ludwig van Beethoven's grandfather was a music teacher. It is not unreasonable to ask whether the element of genius in both sons developed through their upbringing. Beethoven by no means possessed the desired mathematical talent as a German pianist and composer, while at the age of eight, Picasso did not produce a child's drawings but an adult landscape. Neither of these brilliant artists ever paid much heed to academic precision. They never adhered to their era's standard of beauty, yet were responsible for innovation that was far ahead of its time.

In 1901, Picasso began to produce paintings dominated by the colour blue. His work during this 'Blue Period' tended to be gloomy, which meant his career got off to a difficult financial start. The general theme of these paintings was isolation – of human beings in general, but also his own following the suicide of his Spanish friend Carles Casagemas, with whom Picasso shared a studio in Montmartre. In the course of 1902, Paul Gauguin opened Picasso's eyes to the expressive possibilities of the human back. Its vulnerability, together with the passivity of bowed heads and exposed necks, read as an invitation to an Andalusian artist raised on the principle of the domineering man and the submissive woman. This was the period of famous works like *Mother and Child*, *Blue Nude* and *The Old Blind Guitarist*. His painting is less spatial in this Post-Impressionist period, in which he deliberately downplayed the perspective element and experimented with a personal formal language. Picasso's Blue Period marked the beginning of his artistic existence. Afterwards, he would abandon all forms of academic painting. This was the added value with which the twentieth century's most important artist began his career, further inspired by his own isolation. Few appreciated his new style and even fewer responded to the deformed faces in Picasso's later portraits. 'A good painting ought to bristle with razor blades,' he once stated, and the same went for his relationships. Hence the huge variety of his many female portraits, of which *Weeping Woman*, painted in 1937, undoubtedly shows his then mistress Dora Maar. In his art, he sanctified 'flaws' as the only true measure of genius. Picasso was a seismograph for the conflicts, torments and agonies of his age. Petty critics continued to idealize an outmoded, naturalistic approach, lacking as they did any understanding of modern art and rating work entirely on the element of conspicuous technical talent. What had become obsolete, remained for them an ideal. Yet what was new would write history, even while being maligned by the public at large. Labelling something as 'art' should never occur on the basis of creative form alone – it has to embody a higher value if it is to inscribe itself in art history.

Renewal, 'the absolute new beginning', is rarely recognized by the artist's contemporaries. Only those who can see the purity that lies behind it will be able to situate this new art correctly, something that generally only happens much later. Shortly after 1900, Berthe Weill and Alfred Flechtheim were the first to recognize the quality of Picasso's work, followed by Daniel-Henry Kahnweiler, who opened his gallery in Paris in 1907. These are considered to be Picasso's early patrons, who defended his work for the special talent it displayed. Yet there was more to the gigantically creative figure of Pablo Picasso. Small in stature, built like a bullfighter and with scarily penetrating, bulging black eyes, he looked as though he could kill with a glance. There was something impressive and supernatural about him, a charisma that invariably made him the centre of attention. This was an artist who could win over an audience through his personality, even if they barely grasped his work. Following his early success in the gallery world, Picasso quickly adopted the habit of daily meetings to ensure an opportunity to be admired. His secretary provided the organization and Picasso decided, on the morning itself, whether to receive the visitor in a good or a bad mood. Before long, he moved into a majestic building with rooms to match, in which dozens of people waited each day for an audience with the star artist. They came from far and wide and took away tales of their experience. Among the journalists and aristocrats, he was even paid a visit during the Second World War by a curious and awed Nazi.

Christian Zervos, his Greek publisher, who closely tracked Picasso's work from 1929 onwards, published 16,000 works in thirty-three books, chiefly devoted to his paintings (1,885), drawings (7,089) and a body of sketchbooks (4,659). An estimated 50,000 original works are listed in numerous reliable studies, including those of Pierre Daix, Brigitte Baer, Christian Zervos and Diana Widmaier-Picasso, along with David Douglas Duncan's photographic records and the Picasso Project. Picasso was highly productive, became world-famous early on and made a fortune from the sale of an oeuvre that was very widely distributed. As a consequence, a great many art critics will be commenting on his work for decades to come. It is not enough, in other words, to be familiar with an artist's works, you also have to know precisely when they were created. Why and how were they made, and under what circumstances? Only then will the fullest possible documentation be left for posterity, to provide future seekers with a source of knowledge. It is in this way that creators can get in touch more deeply with the viewer/seeker. Conversely, those who help to generalize the notion of art through reference to whatever beauty happens to be popular at a given moment is responsible for a huge misconception that ought better to have been avoided worldwide. Sadly, the whole world today is swamped with art objects – shockingly so. And yet brilliant artists cannot make it to the top without reference to the many creative people who are responsible for this situation. You cannot have a front runner if there is no pack to pull away from.

The Earth has so much to offer and it is here that humanity has undergone our immense evolution. The development of an artistic talent was a necessity from the outset. From the earliest beginnings, human drawings were intended to be empowering, even in the absence of an audience to admire them. Prehistoric humans drew pictures of animals on cave walls as realistically as possible to help locate, corner and kill them and hence ultimately to survive. Their urge for power stimulated their drawing skills and reinforced their real desire. They coloured using pigments from the earth, and they prevailed. Our ancestors already possessed a creative talent and dreamed of power to satisfy their hunger. Humans developed artistic skills and used art to help express that power. The human brain continued to evolve, gaining ever more knowledge and steadily becoming an object of study itself. Forty thousand years later, we classify creatively talented individuals as 'artists' and assign an aesthetic value to their work. Human beings continued to reflect on their needs, knowledge developed and artistic expression emerged in many aspects of life. The culture of building evolved and architects too began to demonstrate their thirst for beauty. In ancient times, temples were decorated in a manner that would radiate power. Talented artisans made stone ornaments and sculpted naturalistic figures, the first in a line of brilliant creations. The Church employed hundreds of thousands of craftsmen, who went on to provide the people with their visual understanding of the Bible. The religious authorities laid down countless injunctions on ecclesiastical design, mythology and biblical scenes, all in accordance with the same pattern. The painters and sculptors in most effective command of their métier helped the Catholic Church to disseminate immense quantities of wooden, stone and painted religious messages. They were not independent artisans with any financial capacity or power of their own, but depended instead on the commissions they were given, which they then executed deferentially and to the letter. They painted, carved and chiselled, creating an immense legacy of visual images. These were the people who shaped fine art, without grand words or personal signatures. The Church's use of art increasingly consolidated it in its power.

For centuries, art was imposed on the people as a religious message, and within this context everything seemed to be a faithful imitation of what was deemed to be 'real'. The Greek philosopher Plato had already criticized this type of 'imitation' four centuries before the birth of Christ. He called it expression without knowledge and considered the work of an artist to be an imitation of reality and hence nothing more than pretence. Artists might imitate many things in stone, wood, silver, gold or paint, Plato argued, but they could not create the subject itself. The key to his criticism of art was that it did not contain sufficient material to elicit the necessary philosophical discourse, leading him to conclude that the art of his time was only a fake form of beauty.

According to Plato, the imitation of reality merely celebrated what already existed and generated a pointless admiration for it. Thousands of years later, the accumulated mass of ancient sculptures and paintings continues to command our admiration. Few things have united, probed and touched so many cultures as art. Art as such is not essential to life, yet it can be an expression of power, as illustrated by the system orchestrated by the Church, which wrote the rules of traditional art history. We have great masses today of brilliantly rendered illustrations, a legacy stemming from the many commissions that were carried out for the most part by skilled artisans whose talents were utterly subservient to the will of the Church. However, even that did not put an end to its evolution. When the Pont Neuf was constructed in Paris between 1578 and 1606, for instance, it was decorated with 381 masks or

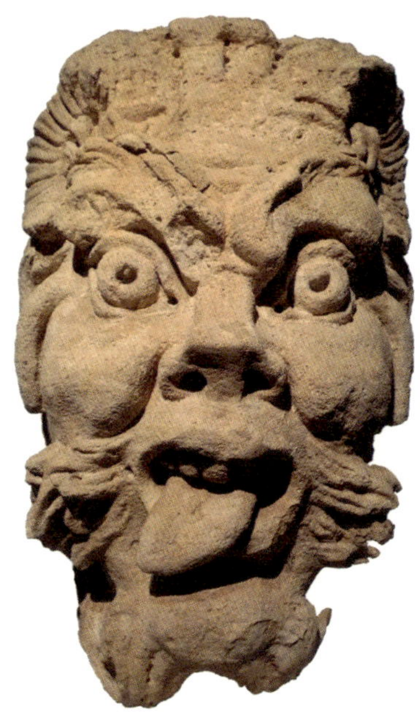

'mascarons' of grimacing satyrs and popular deities, whose irreverent mockery was not an imitation of reality: it took the mind of a sculptor capable of creating these demonic grins, which were very much not things of beauty. When this most famous of Parisian bridges was restored in the nineteenth century, all the satirical images were remade. The original, eroded sculptures are now scattered across private and museum collections.

It all began with the Italian painter Giotto di Bondone (1266/67–1337), whose *Ognissanti Madonna* is one of the earliest works of the Italian Renaissance – an artistic movement that would set the tone for the art world everywhere for a very long time. Painted around 1310, the Byzantine-influenced masterpiece shows the Madonna of all the saints and was done in tempera on a wooden panel measuring 325 cm in height by 204 cm in width. Giotto's painting was just about the earliest aesthetic icon in the history of painting. It was seen as exemplary within the aesthetics of the time and defined what beauty was. The *Ognissanti Madonna* is now a well-protected work that can be admired in all its iconic history at the Gallerie degli Uffizi in Florence.

Works recognized as art at the time were masterpieces of technical ability, yet they were entirely devoted to Christianity, and beneath that layer of seductive gold leaf lay the powerful hand of the Church. Art was religion and religion was power. No matter how talented they were, sculptors and painters of that era were not yet considered to be artists. These artisans lacked the means to develop an artistic expression of their own that would be recognized as such by their contemporaries. Nor, given the pressure of time, was it even straightforward for them to adopt a more authentic and intellectual artistic approach that might yield better results. Yet there were always exceptions. Modern art might have arisen in the nineteenth century, but before proceeding with our argument we can still cite several important pre-modernists – artisans who emerged as artists at an early stage. These were painters whose exceptionally large personalities displayed early signs of autonomy and whose anarchistic streak placed them ahead of their time in an exceptional way.

It was highly unusual for scenes such as those painted by Hieronymus Bosch (c. 1450–1516) to have appeared in the fifteenth century and truly astonishing

Mascaron from the Pont Neuf in Paris, 17th century
Stone, approx. 60 × 40 cm
Abbaye royale de Fontevraud

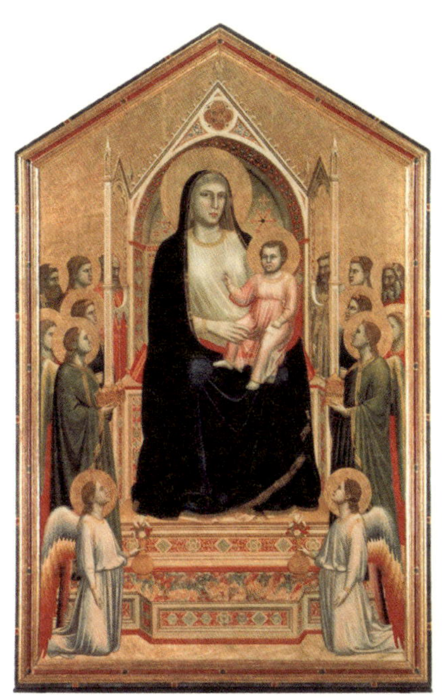

that they survived that era. His paintings were intensely satirical and were given titles such as *The Seven Deadly Sins, The Ship of Fools, The Flood, Visions of the Hereafter* and *The Garden of Earthly Delights*. The objects, colours and themes that Bosch elaborated in his works proved very modern. He revealed himself in his art to be a free citizen and was probably the earliest artist to possess visionary ideas. Bosch made fun of the religious authorities and created all manner of terrifying demons. The themes he painted were diametrically opposed to what the Roman Catholic Church wanted, and few people understood the real message behind his weird scenes. Nicknamed *den duvelmakere* ('the devil-maker'), he offered an incredibly early visual expression of critical ideas that would feature in the sixteenth century in art associated with Protestantism and the Reformation. One wonders, for instance, whether Bosch's *Ship of Fools* was not intended as an allusion to the *festum fatuorum* – an annual festival of fools celebrated in the Middle Ages by the clergy, in which everything the Church had preached for the rest of the year concerning good order, honesty and love for one's fellow human beings was explicitly cast aside. For four days of carnivalesque revelling, the high clergy swapped places with the low, unleashing the collective psyche and giving rise in their intoxication to weird parodies of the Gospels. Senior prelates eventually banned the custom. Bosch's paintings, which likewise survived the 361 other days of the year, when everyone meekly returned to their ecclesiastical duties, combine colourful, contemporary attributes with stories from the Bible and are packed with erotic scenes. His work – which was especially sought after by the nobility – tells us about humanity's folly and hence unmasks human beings and their true nature. Bosch was a sympathizer of the reformist *Devotio moderna* movement and accordingly denounced corrupt practices within the Church. A fascination for the absurd encouraged him to paint the madness of the populace in scenes that still compel our admiration today.

Anchiano, a village near the Italian town of Vinci, was the birthplace in 1452 of the illegitimate child of a young peasant woman and a man named Piero. The infant would later adopt the name of the nearby town as his own. He received a solid if not classical education, but by the age of fourteen, it was already plain that the youngster

Giotto di Bondone
Ognissanti Madonna, c. 1310
Tempera on panel, 325 × 204 cm
Florence, Le Gallerie degli Uffizi

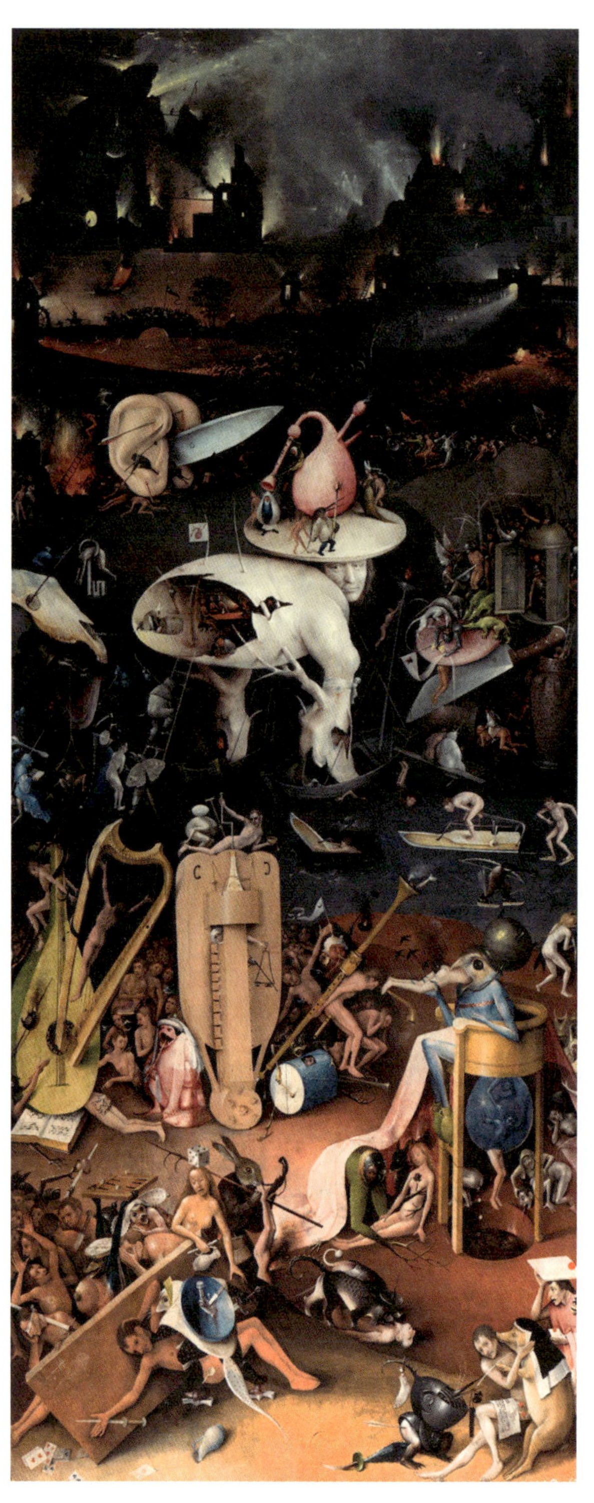

Hieronymus Bosch
Garden of Earthly Delights (right panel), 1490–1500
Oil on panel, 220 × 76.5 cm
Madrid, Museo Nacional del Prado

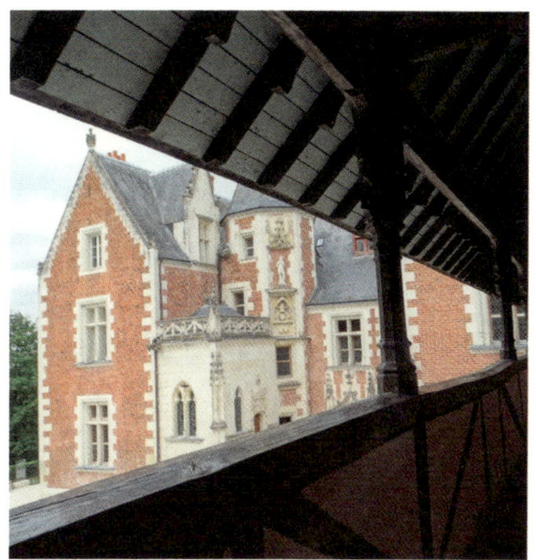

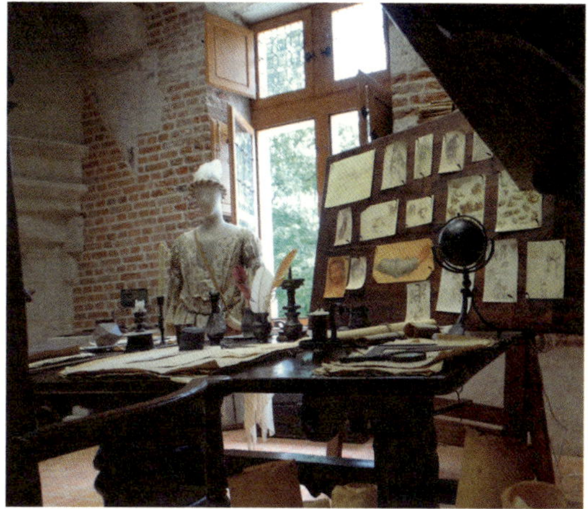

was immense talented. Leonardo da Vinci, figurehead of the Italian Renaissance, went on to become an architect, engineer, inventor, philosopher, physicist, chemist, anatomist, sculptor, writer and painter all at once. He was a humanist with an interest in anatomy, biology, geology, astrology and much more besides. His knowledge and skill were huge and as a *homo universalis* he transcended his time. Leonardo spent the final years of his life at Amboise on the Loire. He owed a great deal to his main patron, Ludovico Sforza, Duke of Milan. In 1516, King Francis I of France invited Leonardo to stay at his Château du Clos Lucé, where he found a new home, study and studio. The possessions he took with him to France included what is now the world-famous portrait *Mona Lisa*. He was a close friend of King Francis I, who used an underground passage linking the Château Royal d'Amboise and Clos Lucé to visit him and discuss his many scientific studies. It is said that the king himself was present when Leonardo da Vinci died on 2 May 1519. He was buried in the Chapelle Saint-Hubert in Amboise.

Leonardo's papers were entrusted to his assistant Francesco Melzi, from whose heirs the sculptor Pompeo Leoni obtained 1,200 mostly technical drawings. He collected them around 1600 in the so-called *Codex Atlanticus*. They include futuristic designs that Leonardo had come up with by the time he was twenty-five, along with anatomical drawings and sketches of mechanical devices, which were later actually realized: the parachute, the helicopter, the machine gun, the diving suit and the tank. Largely types of weaponry, of course, highlighting the fact that genius has not always been about the achievement of beauty, but also a matter of progress, however it might be applied.

Clos Amboise, Château du Clos Lucé

Reconstruction of Leonardo da Vinci's studio, Amboise, Château du Clos Lucé

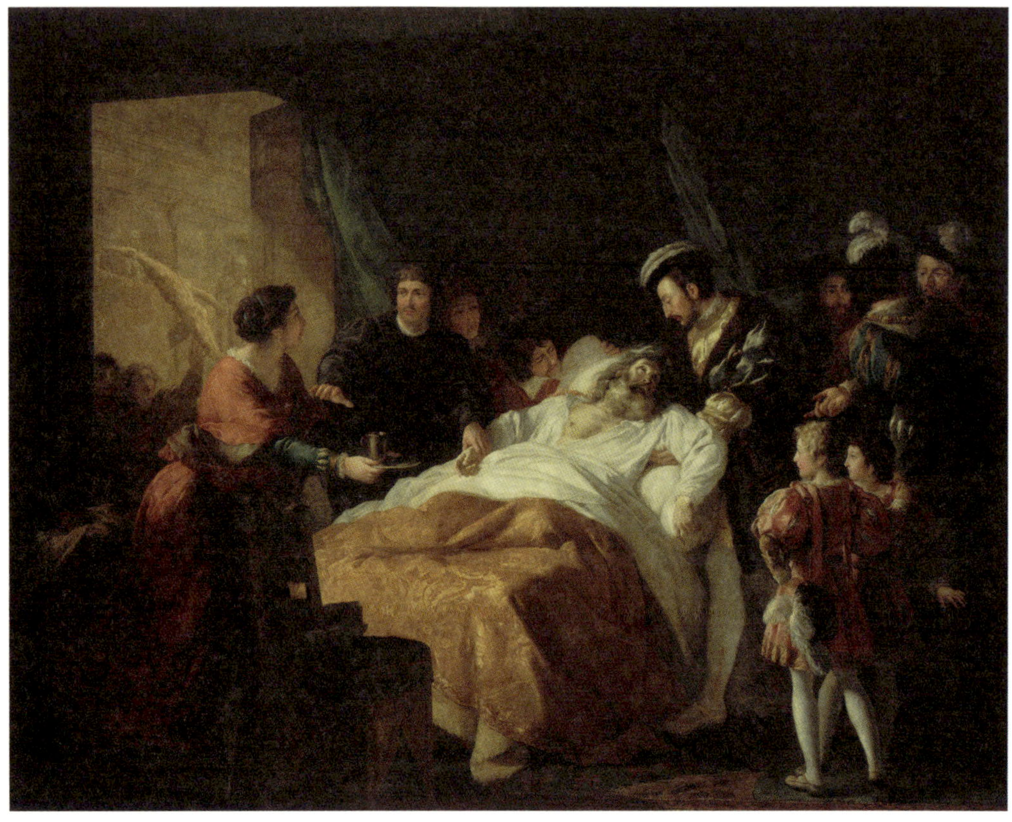

Following on from the demonic fifteenth-century fantasies of Hieronymus Bosch, meanwhile, we can also cite the work of the sixteenth-century painter El Greco (1541–1614). Adopting a free manner of painting, what he depicted was anything but a detailed reality, and was very much at odds with the ossified traditionalism of his time. Drawing a little on our modern art history, it is safe to say that the Cretan painter beat the Expressionists to it by some three centuries. His elongated figures sprang from his imagination and he painted in an intuitive, innovative way. The vivid colour of the figures is accompanied by dramatic shadows. Brutal brushstrokes are smeared across the canvas like cries of anguish. Hands have long, stretched-out fingers without finished nails, while items of clothing are bound together from clods of paint. This exceptionally modern painting technique meant that El Greco served as a powerful example and an inspiring artist in his own day, although his style was subsequently disparaged for many years after his death. El Greco was more than a painter of a scene: he proved himself to be an exceptional artist in terms of both

François-Guillaume Ménageot
Death of Leonardo da Vinci in the Arms of Francis I, 1781
Oil on canvas, 278 × 357 cm
Amboise, Collection du Musée de l'Hôtel de Ville

technique and expression, and did so without regard for the rules imposed by his time. He was a genius who opted for absolute technical and aesthetic freedom and was an expressionist *avant la lettre*. The twentieth-century avant-garde rediscovered and was inspired by his work.

And how do we deal with the beauty behind the mystery of the seventeenth-century sculptor Lorenzo Bernini (1598–1680)? His marble *Ecstasy of St Theresa* is not interpreted by everyone in the same way. Does the Italian sculptor represent true divinity in this sculpture or is the modern era correct in applying its own analysis and declaring the highly polished work of art to be an act of rebellion?

The sculpture shows an angel piercing Theresa's heart with a fiery golden arrow that brings her God's love, prompting us to question the religious dogma of the artist's time through this work. How else can we explain its beauty, as the angel pulls the arrow of love from Theresa's body and observes her reaction? He gazes at her voluptuous, curved pose, eyes closed, lips eagerly parted, at the height of yearning ecstasy, uncontrolled and sensually charged – the very picture of sexual pleasure. In contrast with its more static predecessors, we experience Bernini's theme of union with God as an expressive Baroque drama. Bernini's *Ecstasy of St Theresa* triggered some critical and subversive thinking in the religious context of his time. The perfect realism of his work must have caused a positive shock, its underlying message highlighting the importance of existence. And the manifestation of Theresa's inner ecstasy is surely the very model of a brilliant sensual honesty that uses rationality to free the viewer from all the unbending religious beliefs of the past. With its deep-seated emotion, the now world-famous sculpture reveals the coercion behind the dogma and set the generations that followed thinking.

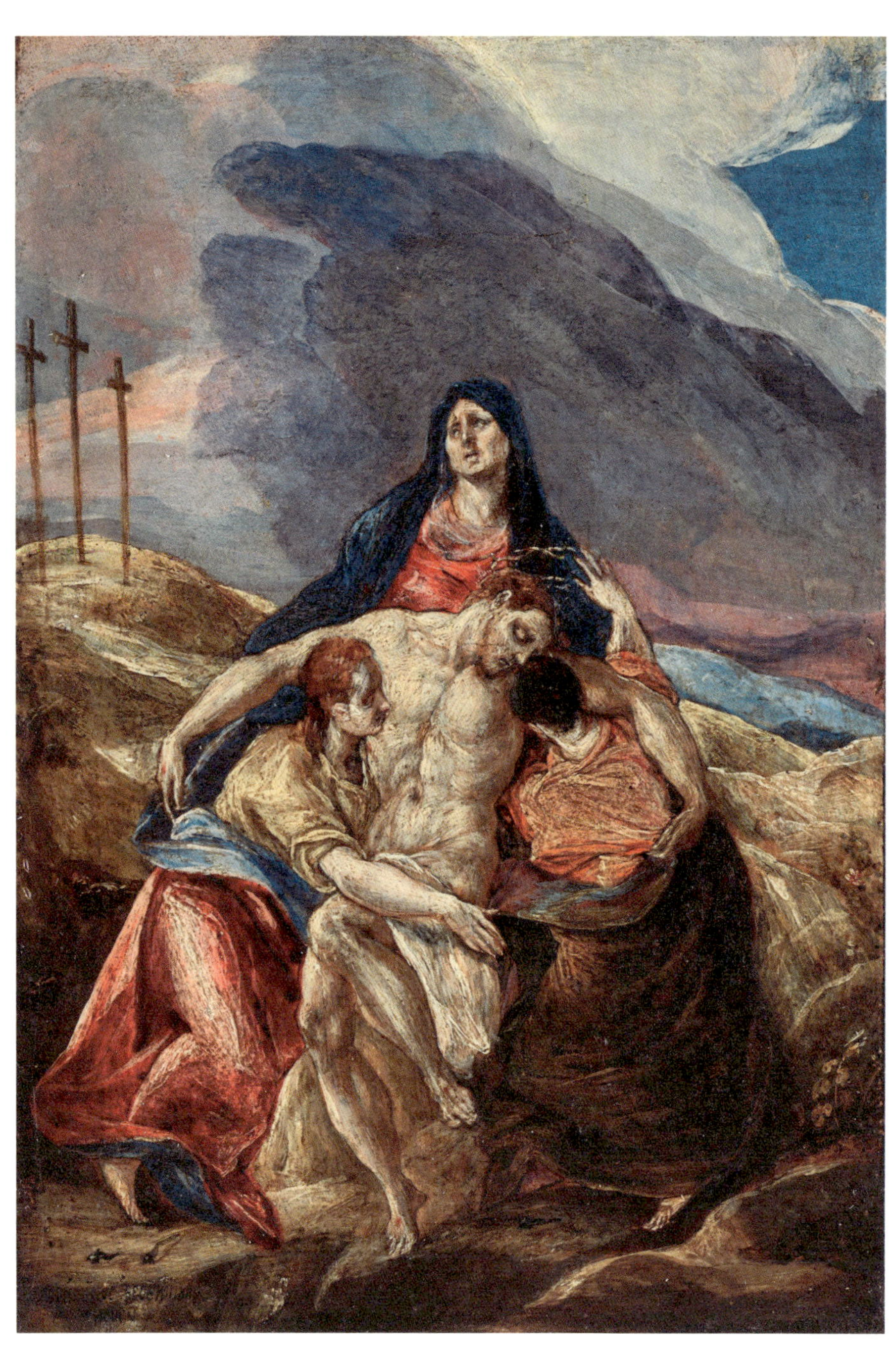

El Greco
Pietà, early 1570s
Tempera on panel, 29 × 20 cm
Philadelphia Museum of Art

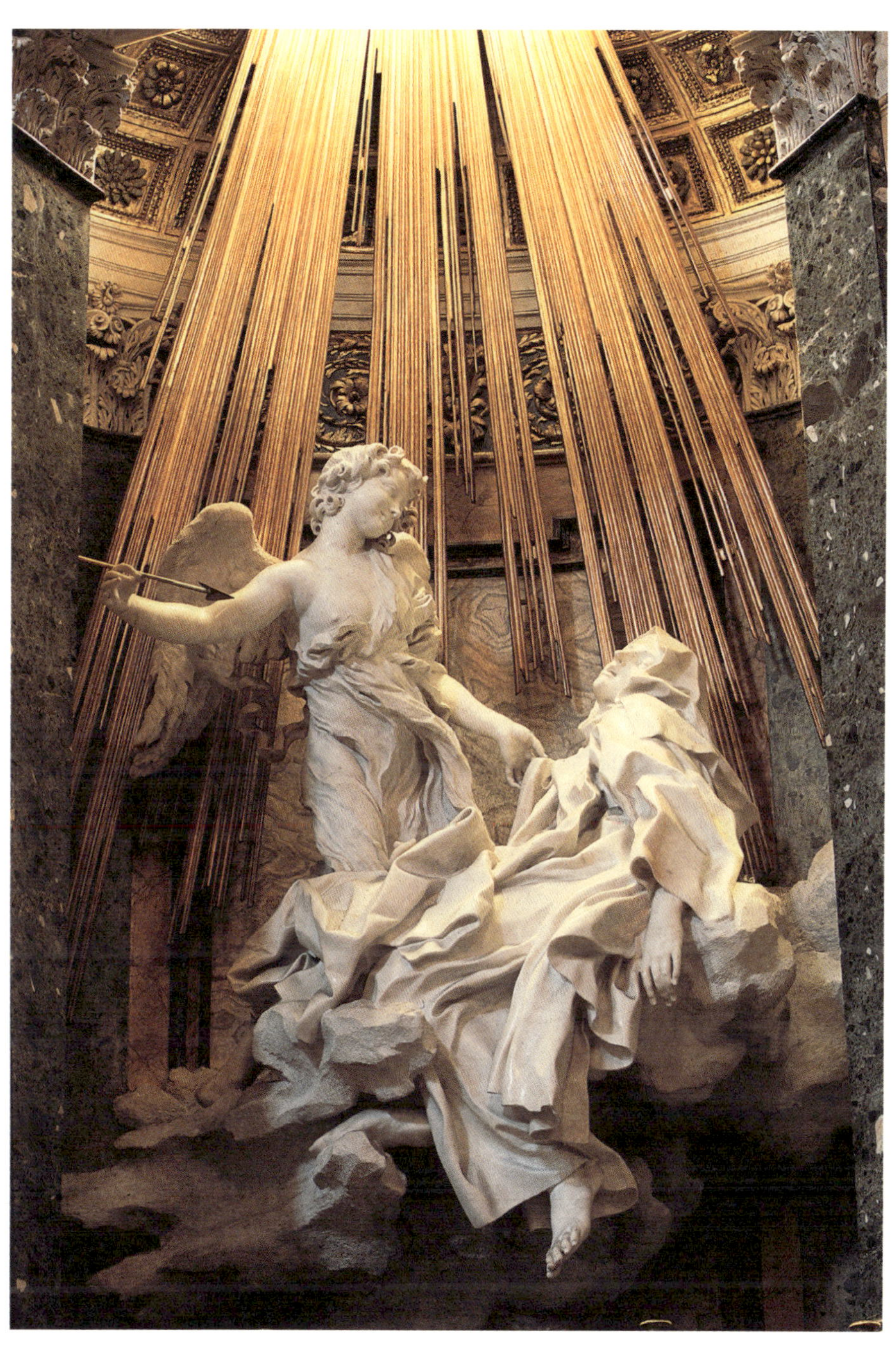

Gian Lorenzo Bernini
Ecstasy of St Theresa, 1647–52
White marble, H 350 cm
Rome, Basilica di Santa Maria della Vittoria

WHEN IT BECOMES ARTISTICALLY ACCEPTABLE TO SHOCK

Time moves on and with it art history, which is necessarily written based on current knowledge. Art history recognizes the inquisitive genius whose oeuvre it then presents in the manner of an official document. These artists have captured what has never previously been recorded. They have taught us how to see and have surprised us. Each of them looked further and, thanks to patrons able to grasp their exploration, what to them was a fresh start became the artistic thinking of the future. Every great artist has stood at a new beginning in the history of art. In other words, art knows no laws: it involves creations that cannot be described or their importance defined in advance. The appreciation of art is likewise constantly evolving within a given period. Art is a sublimated thought so profound that any rebuttal merely affirms the truth of the work. This is why only the greatest artists have sustained their courageous resistance. Their creations survive into the future, guaranteeing them universal attention. And it begins with a handful of patrons who intuit the truth within the furrows of the artist's obstinate evolution. This small history becomes increasingly distinct once the time is ripe to submit to what was hitherto a magnet for scandal. It is this very action/reaction that takes an established undertaking – art – and elevates it to a new beginning. Time writes its history; the focus on the new beginning displaces everything that has gone before; a new generation follows.

Just because unconventional taste does not reach the general public is not to say that popular taste sets the standard for what art ought to be. Art is a cultural tool for interrogating power. It is – or appears to be – innocent, but can ultimately rock the establishment and its many certainties. Art is a necessary and powerful creative reaction against leadership. And yet art and the multifarious opposition it provides has been regarded throughout the ages as a beauty that leads. The world of art functions like a neuron. Artists' brains receive and process the signals, combining them with the rest of their body to develop a language, with which they express themselves and pass on. Nature, which constantly changes their entire environment, offers them enlightenment too. Symmetry might be a golden rule in nature, but not so in art. Beauty as prescribed rule and premeditated perfection is unreliable.

In the eighteenth century, the Enlightenment represented the rebellion of the mind, freedom of thought and a return to nature. This liberal mentality, sceptical by nature, emerged as a new beginning, good for the further general development of society and its art. Scientific discoveries laid the foundations for the industrial revolution that would follow, giving rise to a new wealthy class, the bourgeoisie. The altered living conditions of the newly rich influenced their thinking and encouraged a desire to make art more accessible. This development impacted artists as well, in turn driving a new beginning in art. The supernatural power of religion and Church was countered by a more natural religion, one with an entirely new and more worldly approach, which demonstrated how everything could be different. The Enlightenment stimulated the sciences and placed the emphasis on reason.

Ludwig van Beethoven (1770–1827) did not caress his piano keys in the hope of touching sensitive chords and coaxing hidden tones out of his instrument: he was a musical iconoclast who hammered on his keyboard, as if his scores were the opening salvo of a revolution. He took to the barricades with his first piano concertos, luring music lovers into a new world. This new beginning with entirely avant-garde, dissonant sounds meant that Beethoven was barely understood as a composer at first. Yet by the time of his Ninth Symphony, composed when he was already completely deaf and first performed in Vienna in 1824, he provided the basis for Europe's future national anthem. Without the slightest concession to audience expectations, these were sonic clouds, full of improvisation, abrupt, confused, but with an inchoate power.

The Enlightenment used knowledge and art to lead a culturally hungry public into a freer world. And it did so without any prior formative force. This evolution – which was simultaneously a quest – brought the people to the truth. Art was no longer under the yoke of religious dogma or bound to its cyclical course: a more linear pattern of evolution emerged from 1800 onwards. Industry, education and science evolved; Darwinian ideas were not punished. Free thinking gave rise to a historical consciousness, accompanied and stimulated by the creation of numerous art museums. Artists – painters, sculptors, writers and so on – became the founders during the Enlightenment of a new artistic marketplace, in which there was no longer any room for traditional patronage or sentiment. The Enlightenment brought modernity, while social development meant greater individual freedom and equality. The organization of life and society become more rational and clearer. Art and culture benefited too. The Baroque era ended and the solemn grandeur of Church and nobility made way for Freemasonry, which pursued humanist ideals and universal brotherhood. This new, modern age distanced itself from aesthetic thinking determined by static properties. Art history followed, with the emergence of free art and the unceasing evolution of society, politics and thought. Regional, national and universal artists took to the stage, their level of genius defined by their talent for original expression. Whatever else, the existence of art can be proved by the undeniable fact that you cannot prove it does not exist...

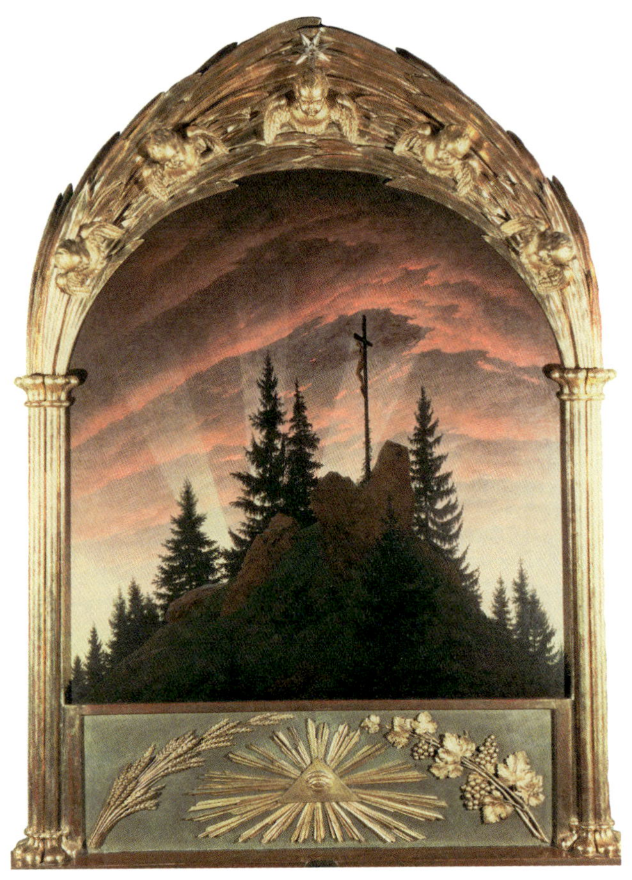

Caspar David Friedrich (1774–1840) was a German landscape painter of the early Romantic period – a movement in Western visual art, literature and music in which subjective spontaneity, introspection and imagination were central. Friedrich's style is no stranger to the Faustian idea of the pact with the devil in exchange for knowledge. He did not paint what was conventionally beautiful, but wild landscapes, sometimes with Gothic ruins and bare trees, or with meditative figures, usually viewed from the back, which draw the viewer into an emotional contemplation of nature, an environment imbued with melancholy. Before creating famous works such as *Wanderer above the Sea of Fog* (1817) and *The Sea of Ice* (1823/24), Friedrich painted *The Cross in the Mountains* (1807/08). Made as an altarpiece, the work focuses on the beauty of nature, with an expressive play of clouds that accentuates the power of Calvary hill. Friedrich included monumental ornamental spruces and placed

Caspar David Friedrich
Cross in the Mountains, 1807/08
Oil on canvas, 115 × 110.5 cm
Dresden, Staatliche Kunstsammlungen

Christ's cross in a spot seemingly cleared of its trees. Less attention is paid to the cross itself. The scene appears deserted. Twigs grow from the shaft of the cross: any religious power loses its raison d'être. The work caused a furore in 1808; Friedrich provoked viewers by breaking with the internal dogma of religious art and elevating landscape above religious image.

The nineteenth century witnessed the rise of modern art against the backdrop of the Industrial Revolution, which had developed half a century earlier in Britain and was now making its way across Europe. Traditional workshops gave way to large factories and art experienced genuine change too. The rise of industry gave artists an opportunity to create much more freely, making use of the era's new materials. The new artists moulded the matter they found and reshaped it into a critical vision of the times. Painters, sculptors and architects were no longer traditional artisans, but inventive artists, leaders and visionaries. They created the 'new image' and called on their viewers for dialogue. Their work grew critical, they unmasked what was customarily expected of art and established a 'new truth' of their own. The public had to reflect: not to be docile but to think critically. Nineteenth-century artists believed that people at large were still subservient to the Church. Art had to address this lie and express an opinion. Belief in a new truth stimulated a further hunger for true art. Those who were creative set a fresh example and encouraged others to distance themselves from beauty as an imposed concept. Artists presented the people with the key to discover all they did not yet know. Intellectual receptivity emerged as a spiritual value and the new attitude would energize art and shape its essence forever.

Serious illness left Francisco de Goya (1746–1828) deaf at the age of forty-seven. His poor health meant that he lived in constant fear of death, rendering his work darker and more critical of social and political issues. War had embittered him so much that he rounded off his career with a series of 'Black Paintings', including *Saturn Devouring His Son* (1820–23).

Modern art and anarchism are inseparably linked. Goya's run of anarchistic work began with *The Third of May 1808 in Madrid* (1814). The title of the now world-famous painting recalls a horrific date: Goya's painting of the mass execution of Madrid citizens by Napoleon's army during the Spanish War of Independence is the first revolutionary image in the history of art. It is revolutionary in every sense: in style, subject matter and the goal the artist had in mind. The content, presentation and emotional power of the work were groundbreaking and it became an archetypal image of the horrors of war. Goya took the highly innovative step of placing a figure in a white robe among a group of terrified citizens awaiting their execution. The man adopts the pose of Christ nailed to the cross, his hands even showing stigmata. The French government had ordered its troops to execute a group of dissidents,

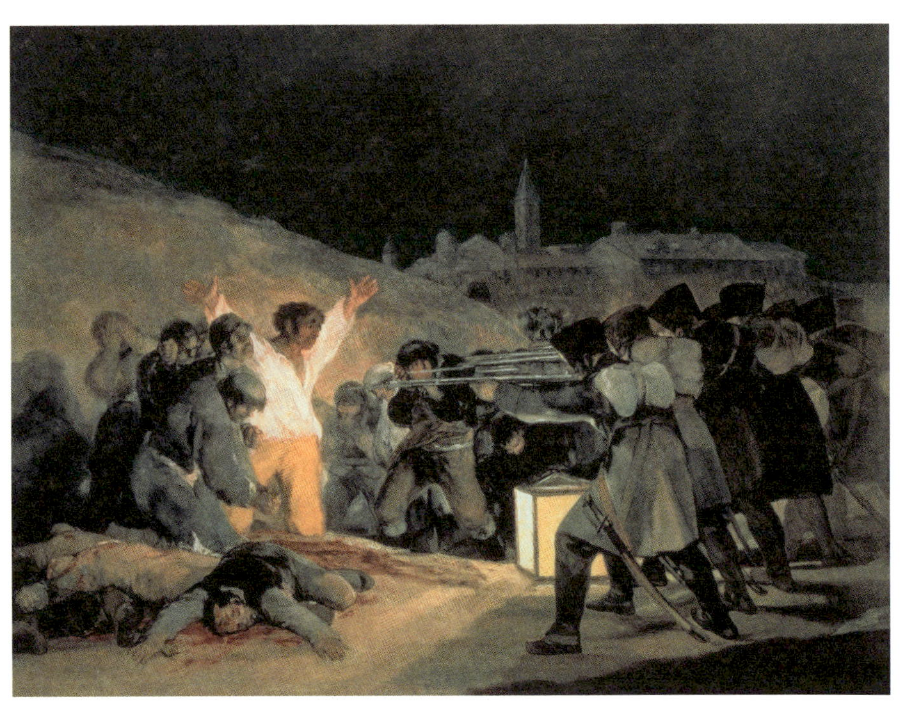

Francisco de Goya
The Third of May 1808 in Madrid, 1814
Oil on canvas, 268 × 347 cm
Madrid, Museo Nacional del Prado

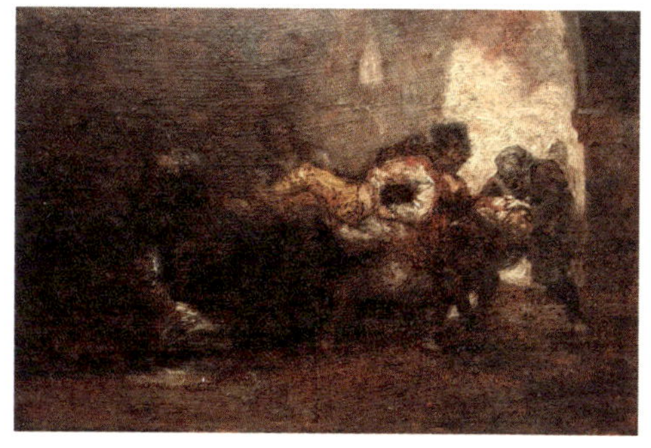

for whom Goya's sympathy is palpable. He made a clear break here with convention, the traditions of Christian art and previous representations of war. Goya was the first artist to criticize the pursuit of power, making his message a controversial one and establishing him as a key figure in the history of anarchism in art. The figure in the white robe was 'his' Christ figure – symbolizing a critical attitude towards the Catholic world and calling on people not to kill their fellow human beings. In contrast to its counterpart *The Second of May 1808*, it is a resolutely anti-heroic work that depicts cruelty and fear of death.

After 1808, Goya painted a similar small canvas with the title *Carrying the Wounded*. It was done around the same time and in a similar spirit to the aforementioned masterpiece, and is also related in terms of its presentation. Its theme – the transfer of casualties – reiterates both the opposition of ordinary people to their warmongering government and the artist's revolutionary ideas. Through the central figure in the white shirt and yellow trousers, Goya, the figurehead of pure anarchism in art, suggests that the rescue of the wounded shows the people's unflagging resistance to the executions. The central figure, meanwhile, is once again a symbol of the immortal Christ. In this way, Goya became the first artist to paint the dramatic side of war as an irrational act of suffering, pain and death. His criticism contrasted sharply with those other painters whose work served as propaganda, glorifying the conquerors on their thrones. Goya was the creator of the figure with arms outstretched as if nailed to a cross, yet simultaneously the martyr seeking to give the people hope. His small oil painting of the wounded principal figure also led to the series of eighty-two prints titled *The Disasters of War*, produced between 1810 and 1820, and which are likewise closely related to the themes of the more famous painting.

Another German philosopher – Georg Wilhelm Friedrich Hegel (1770–1831) this time – also changed the way art is perceived. Unlike Kant, he did not discern any connection between the beauty of nature and the beauty of art. Hegel did his thinking in the period that saw the first anarchistic work of art, courtesy of Francisco de Goya, and this is clearly discernible in his philosophy. To his mind, the only arts that qualified as 'fine' were born of a process of thinking. Art is not what you see, but what you think. Only then does it have a function. Hegel's thesis destroyed the principle underlying the Renaissance, whose great master, Leonardo da Vinci, once wrote: 'Art lives from constraints and dies from freedom.' This assertion, typical of

Francisco de Goya
Carrying the Wounded, 1808–14
Oil on canvas, 20.5 × 30.5 cm
Private collection

its time, had been discarded by the nineteenth century, by which time Leonardo's principle had entirely disappeared, to be replaced without demur by Hegel's conviction that art must arise in 'a stage of the spirit' in precisely the same way as philosophy. Art to Hegel has nothing to do with beauty, taste or adherence to the Church's rules. Judgement of taste gives way to the external aspect: what we see no longer exists for the sake of the absolute conception of art. Hegel's vision played a vital role in innovative philosophical thinking in the nineteenth century and is also clearly reflected in Goya's *Third of May 1808 in Madrid*. The latter work is likely to have been a model for Eugène Delacroix too, who had the courage in turn to create *Liberty Guiding the People* in 1830. This was the first time that the world of art made its mark on the struggle for democracy: power to the people!

All the old dogmas had been jettisoned before the twentieth century; the world of art was changing both visibly and radically, while loudly proclaiming its new truth. The judgement of taste as a measure of beauty had to go, while the painting of nature ceased to be synonymous with the straightforward depiction of natural forms 'as they are'. Artists no longer felt any need to stick to the well-trodden path, to follow the ideas of previous generations. Art distanced itself from a general imperative –now pointless and obsolete – to create conventional beauty. A need for greater intellectual depth and a more progressive gaze now became the priority. In a clear departure from the past, modern artists were attentive to their new generation and offered art lovers the language of the future. Goya's *Third of May 1808 in Madrid* vilified the murderous treatment of the Spanish people; in 1830, Eugène Delacroix painted the activist Marianne as a symbol of the fight for freedom; while in 1868, Edouard Manet's *Execution of Maximilian* was an indictment of the French emperor. With its undertone of criticism, this modern art offered viewers a fresh perspective, a different way of seeing the world. The artists who created it were, in turn, forerunners of what the next century would have to offer.

The art world in the 1980s was introduced to the work of Keith Haring (1958–1990), whose brush drawings represented a new beginning for art and for society alike. The new forms with which the young American addressed a specific set of issues was highly unusual for the time. Haring's work looks amusing, but is much more than that. His art frequently carries a message. It demands the viewer's attention and calls loudly for the acceptance of homosexuality. *Dancing Boys* (1981), for instance, is a piece on pink paper in which naked, dancing youths are connected by their penises. It was followed by a series of cartoonish penises that the artist turned into walking or winged figures. From 1984 onwards, however, many of his subjects related to death. Haring contracted AIDS, for which there was no treatment at the time. He focused on it increasingly as a theme until the end of his life. His love

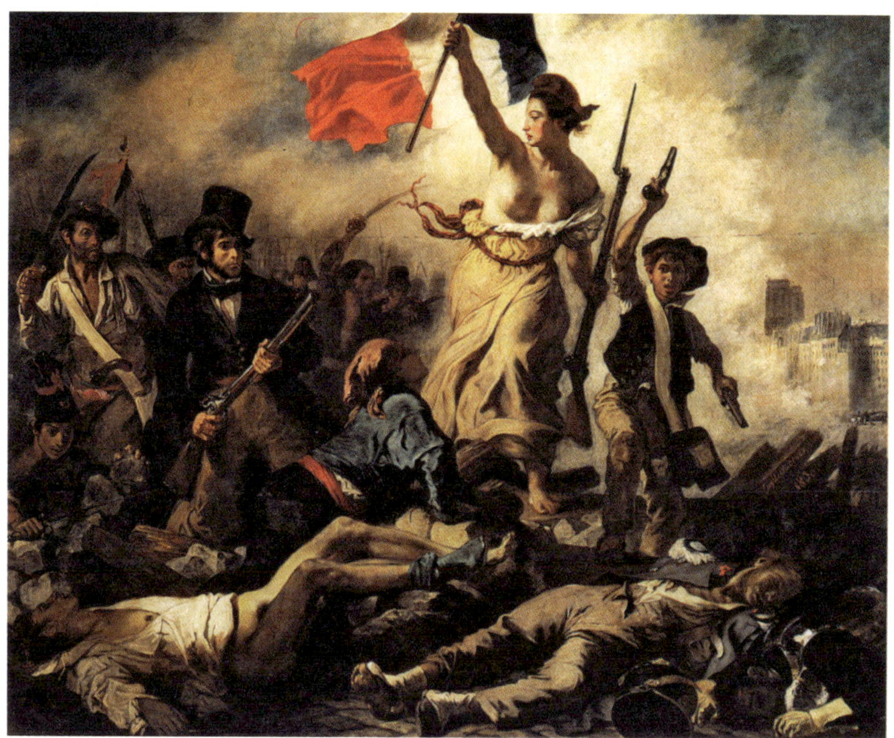

of his own sex and of art made his painted messages a clarion call for understanding of the LGBT+ community. Strange as it seems, the drawings of Asclepius's snakes, prison bars, hands bound together, crosses, spitting monsters and scissors severing lifelines were all cheerful drawings on the theme of death. As the end of his life loomed, Haring continued to proclaim the sad message that runs like a thread through his work. To this day, there are many societies around the world in which homosexuality is not accepted.

Many of today's artists are likewise profoundly engaged with the issues of our time, through which they hope to exert some positive creative influence. Banksy, the British artist who prefers to keep his identity secret, is one such current trigger. The fact that he remains incognito and works in this way around the world has had an exceptional impact on what he creates. His art is radically new, both physically and thematically. Banksy uses a quickfire stencil and aerosol technique to inscribe his ideas in the streetscape and to express his political, cultural and ethical commitment. His work is socially engaged and communicative at street level, with a simplicity that is strikingly original and arresting in its content. Those with a guilty conscience can

Eugène Delacroix
Liberty Guiding the People, 1830
Oil on canvas, 260 × 325 cm
Paris, Musée du Louvre

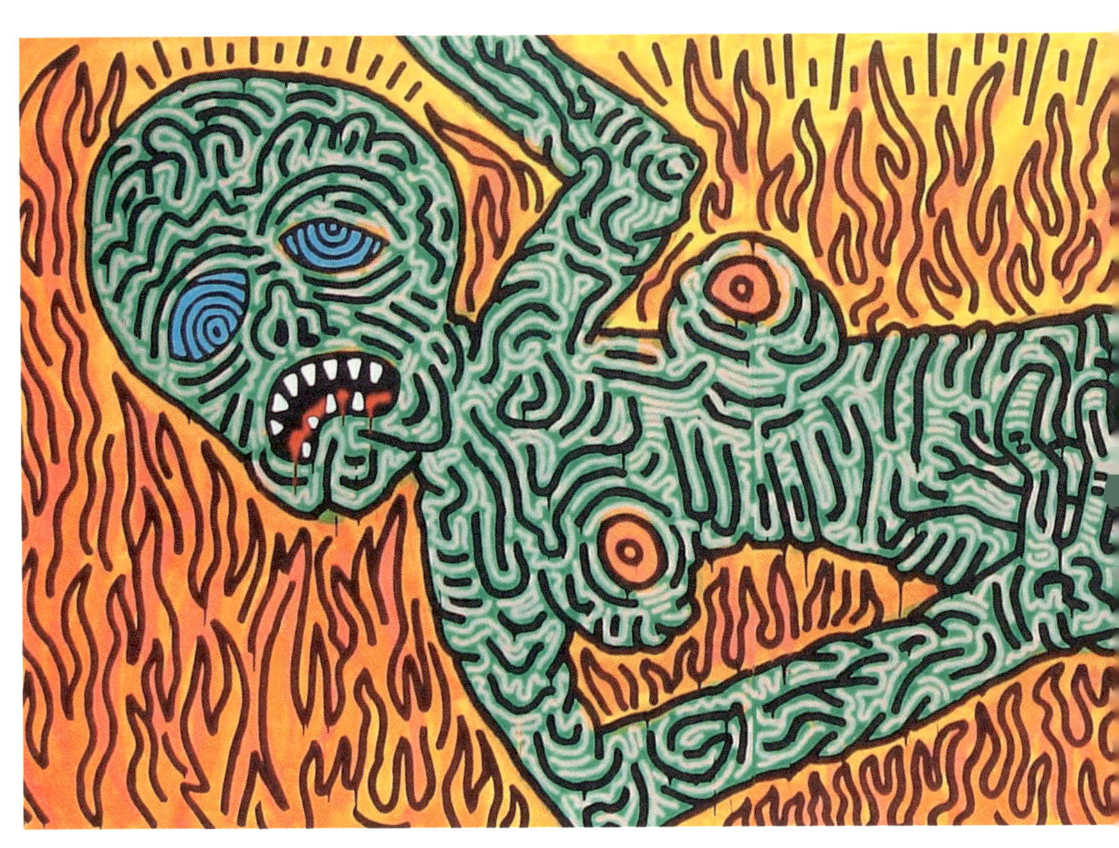

Keith Haring
Heaven and Hell, 1984
Acrylic paint on canvas, 457 × 152 cm
International Modern Art Foundation Belgium

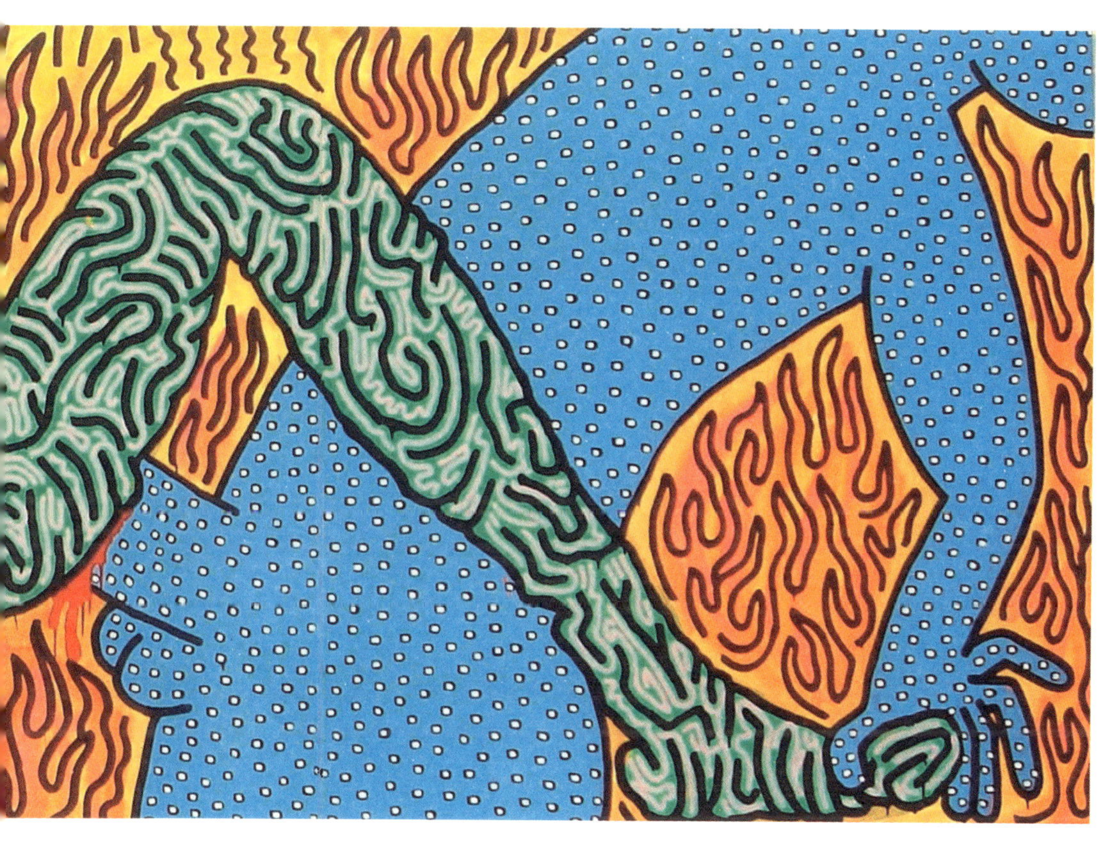

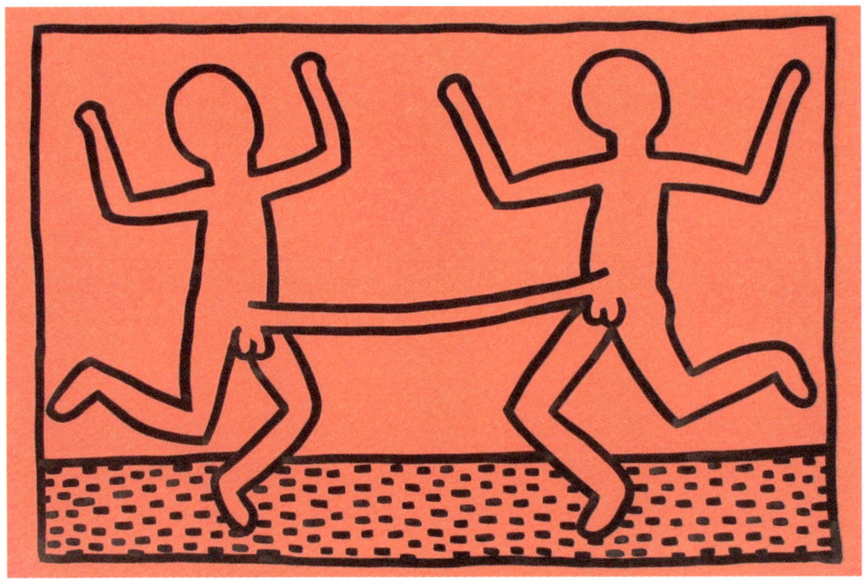

reflect on it, while those who share his opinion can pass it on. Banksy's art reaches a mass audience, with which it goes down very well. Never has an artist addressed the general public worldwide in such a simple, logical and innovative way. He gives the establishment a kick up the backside. The Banksy approach would have lent itself equally well to criticism of the execution of the Spanish citizens and that of Maximilian, or in support of democracy, as symbolized by the banner with which Marianne heralded the arrival of the 1830s.

His art might seem playful, but his message is highly critical and far from cheery. *Smiling Cop* (2003), for example, depicts a heavily armed policeman with a smiley face. From a Belgian perspective, the officer was not a realistic street figure at the time, but would prove visionary thirteen years later when a military force, guns at the ready, was deployed in major cities following the terrorist attack on Brussels Airport. To us, at least, the *Smiling Cop* was a reality *avant la lettre*. His visionary creation was in the interest of society and he represented an important message that we ought to believe. An image of a police officer with a gun and an expressive smiley face for a head is a significant piece of graffiti art in a period of terrorism and the spectacle of war. The fact that (for Belgians like myself) this fantasy would be transformed into reality lay entirely in the spirit of the artwork itself: an example of contemporary art with a raison d'être. Art must be seen, analysed and heard. The proof of art is that it exists.

Keith Haring
Dancing Boys, 1981
Sumi ink on paper, 58.2 x 88.2 cm
International Modern Art Foundation Belgium

Banksy came to the forefront of the current and universal history of art on 5 October 2018 with a piece of theatrical art terrorism inflicted on the buyer of his *Girl with Balloon*. The work was auctioned with a guide price of €221,000–332,000, but sold for just under €1.5m. At the moment the sale was finalized, with the audience looking on, the work was pulled down into its bombastic frame and through an ingeniously disguised shredder. *Girl with Balloon* was a piece of anti-capitalist performance art, an act devised by the artist himself. Banksy created a shock by shredding an expensive artwork and thus mocking the contemporary art trade, which buys through word of mouth rather than using its eyes. After Banksy's stunt, he retitled the sold work as *Love Is in the Bin*. Yet while the artist himself might have consigned his work to the garbage, the art market thought otherwise: the now world-famous shredded million-and-half euros proved to be a great investment for its new owner. He was not a collector with any deep love of art and did not cherish the art-historical statement either. For him, art was cash and he promptly flipped his shredded icon. Sotheby's in London slapped a new guide price of €4–7m on the remains of Banksy's statement, but yet again investor adrenaline drove the closing price even higher. Despite being known for his anti-capitalist advocacy, Banksy bestowed a fresh meaning on this controversial work through the act of shredding it. In the end, an artwork whose maker had assigned it to the bin went for €22m.

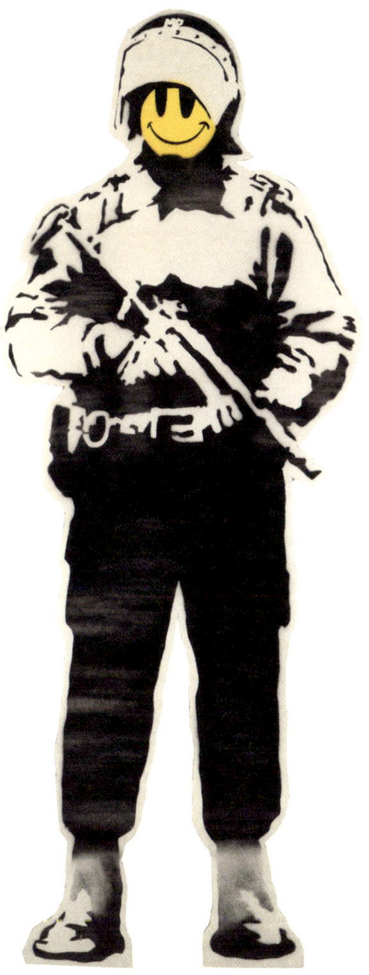

Banksy's universal success had earlier resulted in a legal battle concerning the intellectual property rights to his designs. A shady art dealer realized there was money to be made from these spray paintings and started to place Banksy's messages on all sorts of materials. Pest Control – Banksy's legal representatives – sued, but lost the trademark rights on the grounds that anonymity has no legal standing. According to the judge, Banksy's rights could not be defended since it was not clear who Banksy was or whether such a person even existed. The defendant could not have violated the trademark, which Banksy had filed some years earlier, since the right was held by a person who declined to prove that he existed. As a result, Pest Control was

Banksy
Smiling Cop, 2003
Spray paint on cardboard, 200 × 78 cm
International Modern Art Foundation Belgium

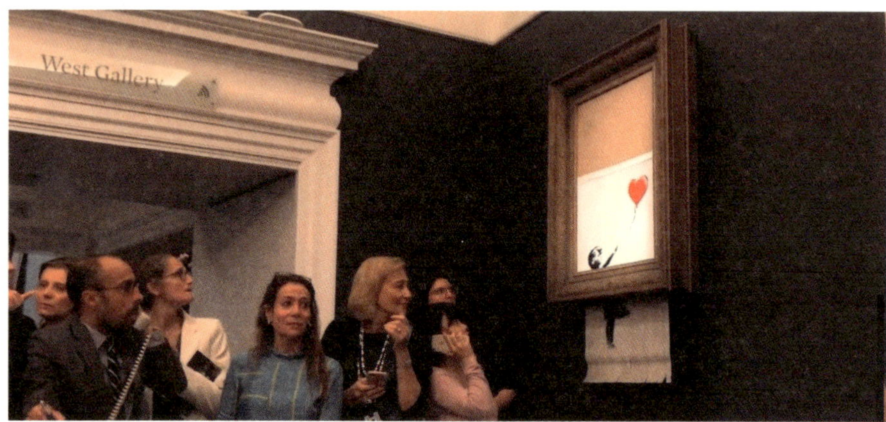

likewise deemed not to be a legitimate agent. Banksy preferred to remain invisible throughout. As one of his spray paintings had once proclaimed: 'Copyright is for losers'.

THE NEW BEGINNING

Thinking about art thus began to change around the time of Francisco de Goya's gruesome works. The rules ceased to apply and the art world bade farewell to the received conception of beauty, in which a perfect finish was all that mattered. According to this 'new beginning', real art is not an expression of beauty at all, but conveys a message, an expression of the mind. Henceforth, the enjoyment of art would primarily be a matter of reason, with technical perfection gradually becoming secondary. Art had evolved and it also demanded that its beholders open their minds to its new understanding. A work of art that expresses horror requires reflection on the viewer's part in order to intrigue, and this is not a straightforward matter for anyone not especially keen on art. From now on, it was reason that determined what art was – an art that many people perceived as ugly. Few at the time will have found

Auction of *Girl with Balloon* at Sotheby's in London, 5 October 2018

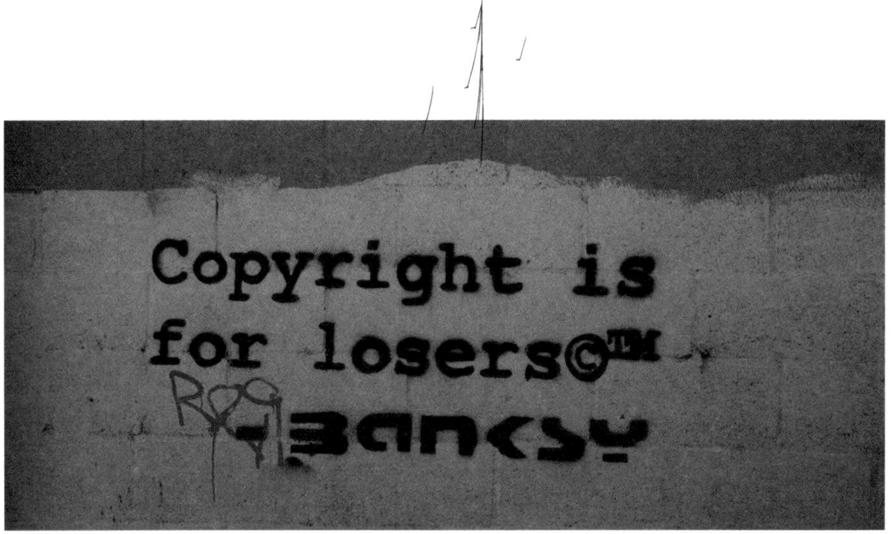

Goya's *Third of May 1808 in Madrid* to be beautiful. What Spaniard could relish a painting in which a firing squad executes a group of people, and in the very country where the scene had taken place? From the beginning of the nineteenth century, the judgement of beauty became subordinate to the goal that art had in mind. Artists no longer seduced their viewers with an aesthetically pleasing image or an urge for beauty, but obliged them to acquire knowledge and to seek the real meaning that lay behind the image. Those who broke with artistic tradition in a revolutionary way – as either individuals or a group – were thus oblivious to criticism. They were innovators both stylistically and in terms of their social critique and did not wish to be dependent any longer on a specific movement in art. These artists were driven by the absolute necessity of expressing their ideas about the world, and as such brought about a change in the art world. Avant-gardists like this invariably caused offence in their own time and so can no longer be considered craftsmen either.

Political anarchy was first apparent, therefore, in the work of Goya, Edouard Manet and Eugène Delacroix. It arose through their innovative ideas, which set the example in turn for other avant-gardes that followed later, such as Divisionism, Cubism, Futurism, Dadaism, Constructivism, Suprematism and Surrealism. Each of these movements had pioneers of its own, in terms of content and style – revolutionary artists who rejected the conventions of the bourgeois and the academic. In January 1937, the Spanish government asked Pablo Picasso to paint a large work for the upcoming World Exhibition in Paris. He responded with a monochrome canvas centring on political anarchy. The Republicans were less than keen on the anti-fascist *Guernica* – a monumental painting in which Picasso expressed his disgust at the German-Italian bombing raid that had wiped the eponymous Spanish town off the

Banksy
Copyright is for Losers, 2007
Spray paint on wall, dimensions and location unknown

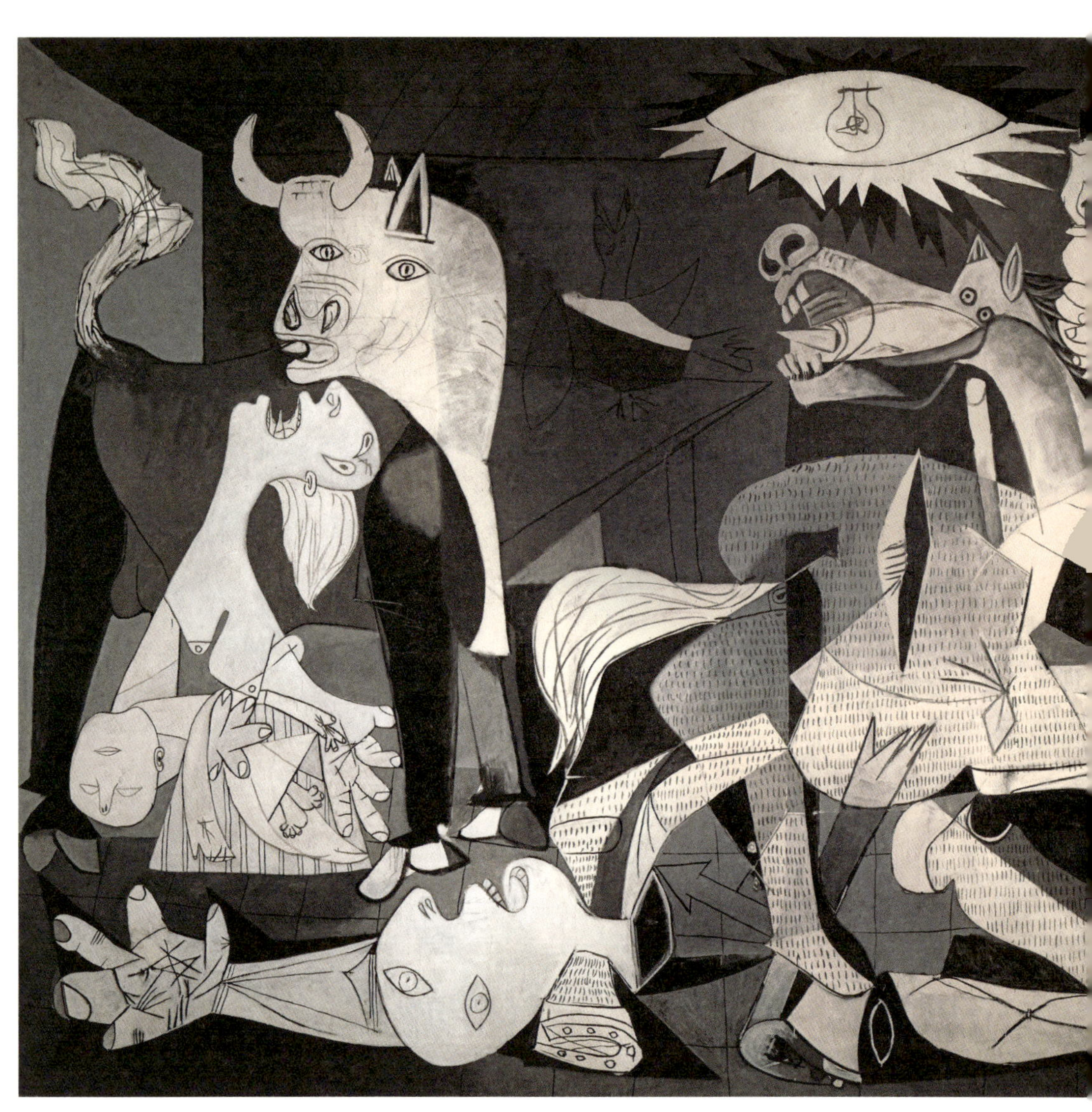

Pablo Picasso
Guernica, 1937
Oil on canvas, 349.3 × 776.6 cm
Madrid, Museo Nacional Centro de Arte Reina Sofia

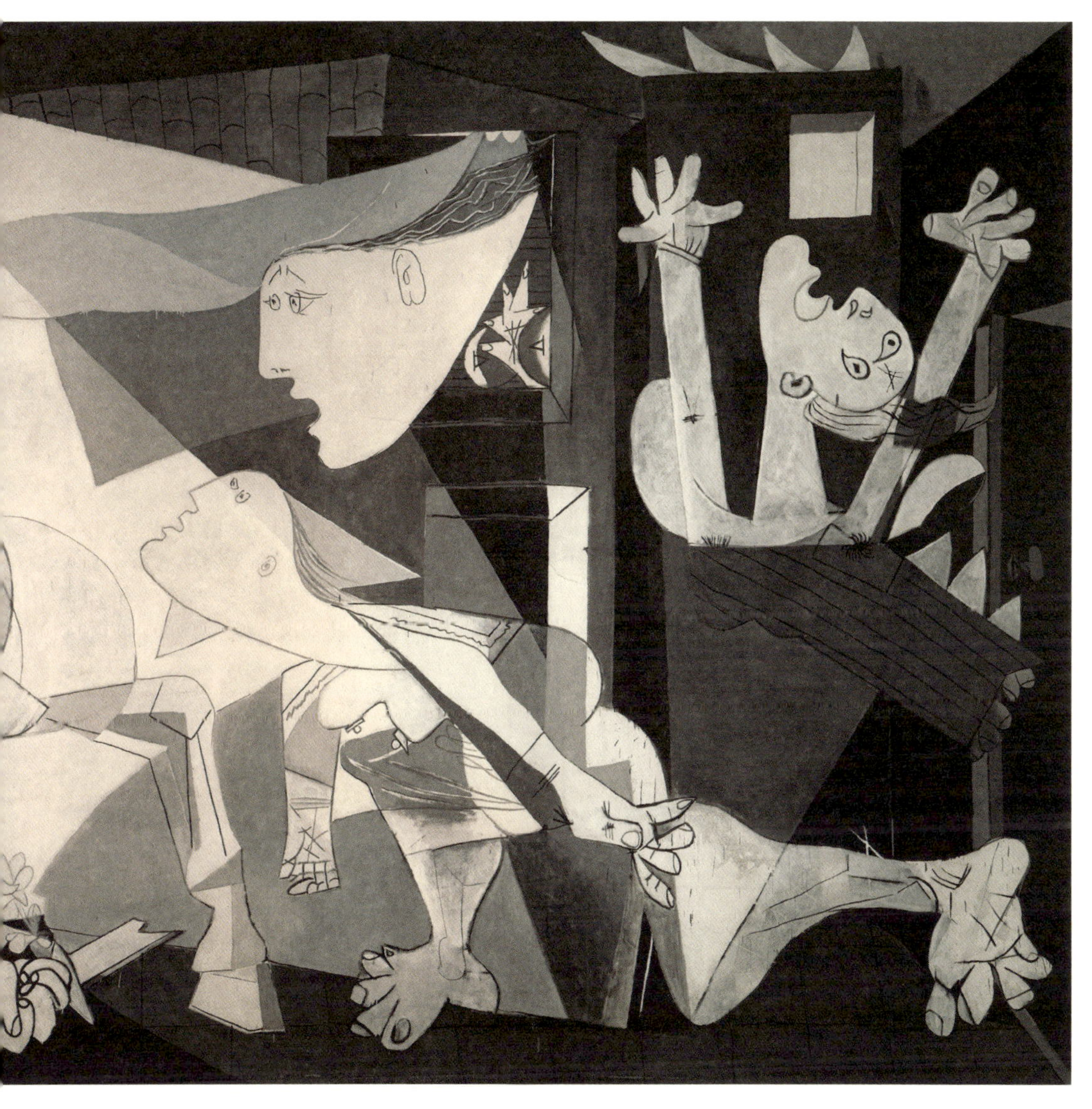

map. The attack occurred during the Spanish Civil War, fought between 1936 and 1939. On the day Francisco Franco proclaimed the end of the war in Burgos, 1 April 1939, Picasso swore never again to set foot on Spanish soil as long as the dictator remained in power. True to his word, he never did return to Spain. The now world-famous *Guernica* can be seen today at the Museo Reina Sofía in Madrid. Despite the ban placed on the artist by the Franco regime, a collection was founded in Barcelona in 1963 that would later form the basis of the Museu Picasso, with thirty-five rooms displaying over four thousand of the artist's works. Picasso died in 1973, two years before the dictator Franco.

The French term 'avant-garde' originated in the twelfth century. Soldiers in this 'vanguard' or 'advance guard' were sent ahead to reconnoitre the battleground and engage the enemy first, which meant they risked being cut to pieces. Much later, the term began to be applied in the art world too, in which avant-garde artists were equally exposed: they were likewise at the forefront, proclaiming their truth and forming a 'new beginning'. The term 'avant-garde' can certainly be applied to what Hieronymus Bosch achieved in the fifteenth century with his demonic fantasies. His subject matter meant that he risked being burned as a heretic, a fate he was miraculously able to avoid. And what about El Greco? He too can be considered a very early artistic innovator. Yet many artisan-painters of his era viewed the Greek with his avant-garde ideas as a failed artist. There were few in the Renaissance era who were prepared to accept his new style. El Greco painted in a manner all his own and paid no heed whatsoever to conventions, either aesthetic or technical. He had the courage to embark on an entirely personal 'new beginning' in his era, depicting suffering figures in a highly expressionistic way: stretched out and dressed in garments consisting of clumps of paint. Not to mention clouds of a kind that would not return to startle the art world until the arrival of Emil Nolde at the beginning of the twentieth century. Despite painting outside the boundaries of all customary norms, El Greco realized an admirable body of art for which he would only be recognized much later.

Another artist who delivered a visual corrective to his time was Egon Schiele (1890–1918), with his plastic watercolours of female bodies. In 1910, he took women in provocative poses and an erotic frankness to the brink of pure pornography. Solitary masturbating women and intertwined girls dressed only in brightly coloured stockings were common themes. With their fixed gaze and naked bodies convulsed with pleasure, Schiele's women experience a sensual climax. His erotic drawings were dreamlike fragments of shameless honesty, collected in a mixture of exciting, colourful contrasts, in which burgeoning sexuality evoked lust and desire. His artistic expression posits itself as a reality, asserts a proposition. The ultimate in

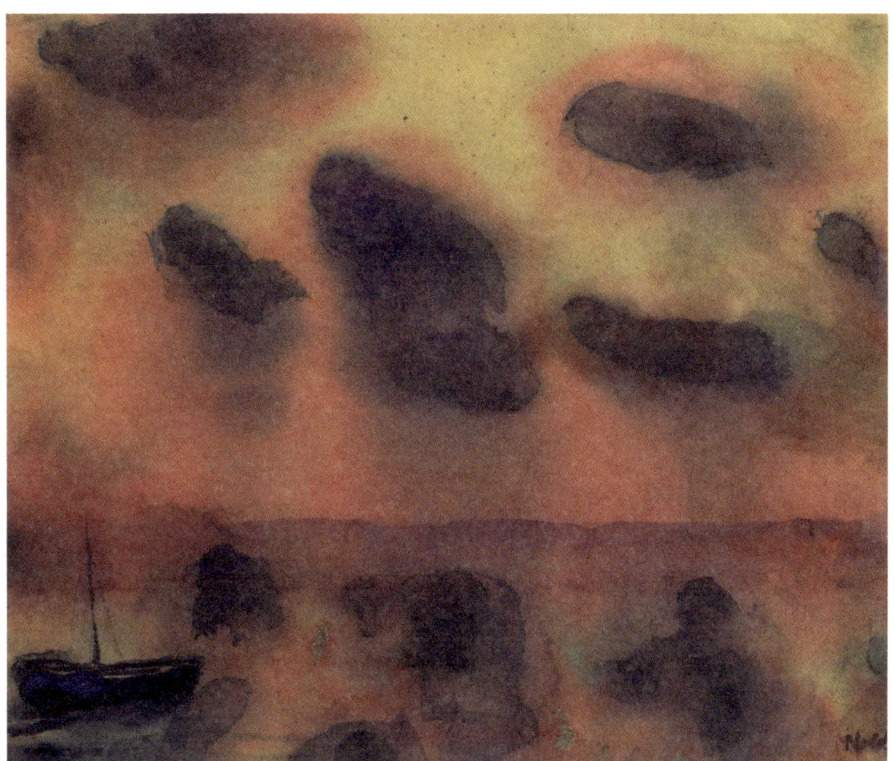

beauty arises from the confrontation with it, which can also be shocking if the viewer does not acknowledge that reality. Brilliant art invariably balances on this narrow line, making it universal and ageless, because of which the moving drama that Egon Schiele expresses in his work is honest and truthful. His work reflects his times in an unusually captivating expression of life, wrapped up in an aesthetic message that is provocatively sincere.

Great artists do not censor and they spontaneously express what they think or feel as an individual. If, by contrast, they set out to pander to their viewers by creating an excellent work for them, the result will be the very definition of what is no longer acceptable as art: art calls for boundaries to be pushed. Artists who want to achieve fame in their own lifetime are self-deadening. Their craving for success turns them into something other than who they really are, a state of affairs that no true artist could ever want. When artists strive for immediate success, they do so by creating what the general public will consider 'beautiful'. Artisanal creators who produced work of this kind will never achieve their full potential. Not to mention the

Emil Nolde
Seascape with Boat, 1946
Watercolour on Japanese paper, 22.6 × 27 cm
International Modern Art Foundation Belgium

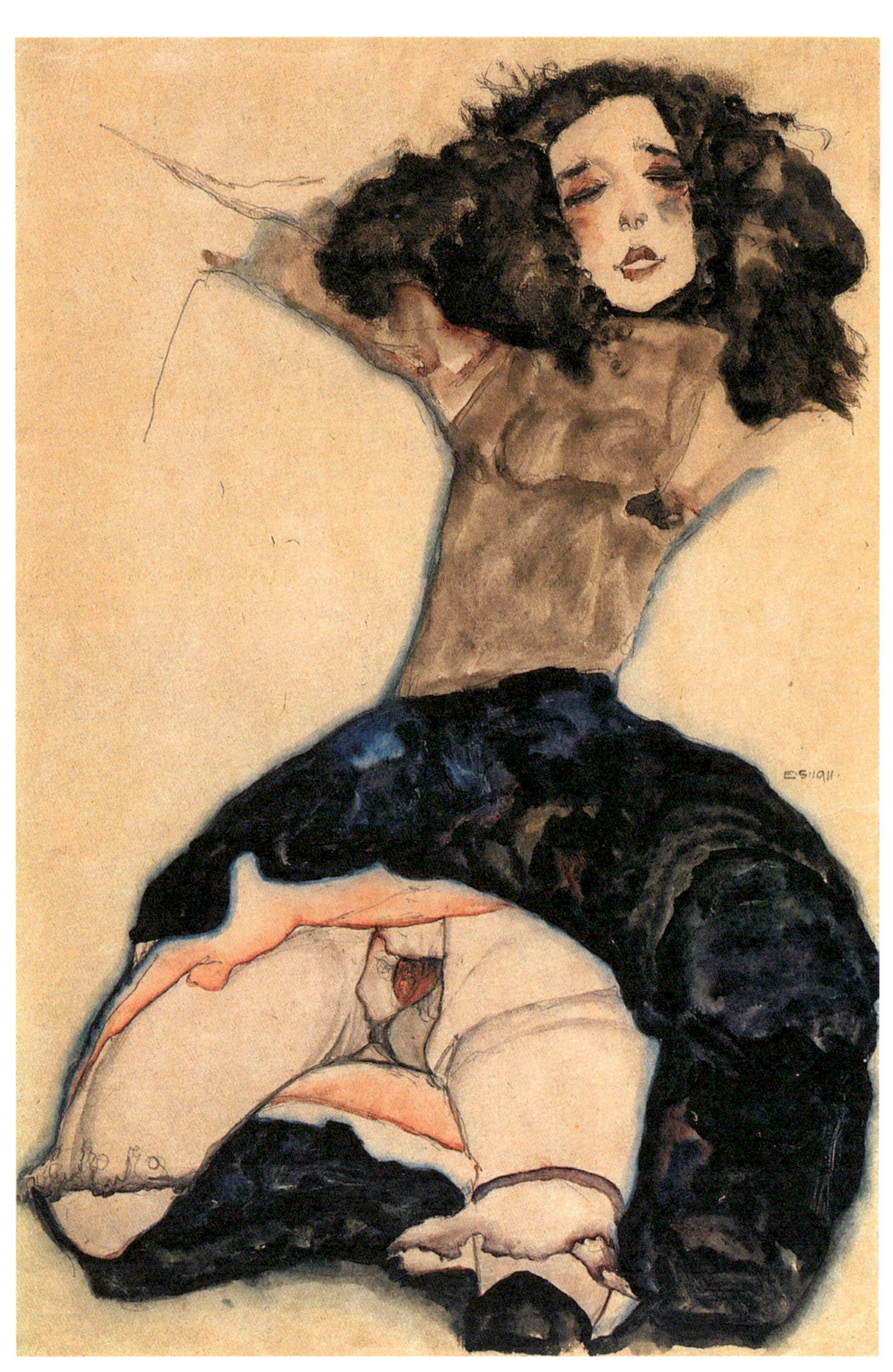

Egon Schiele
Black-Haired Girl with Lifted Skirt, 1911
Gouache, watercolour and pencil on paper, 55.8 × 37.9 cm
Vienna, Leopold Museum

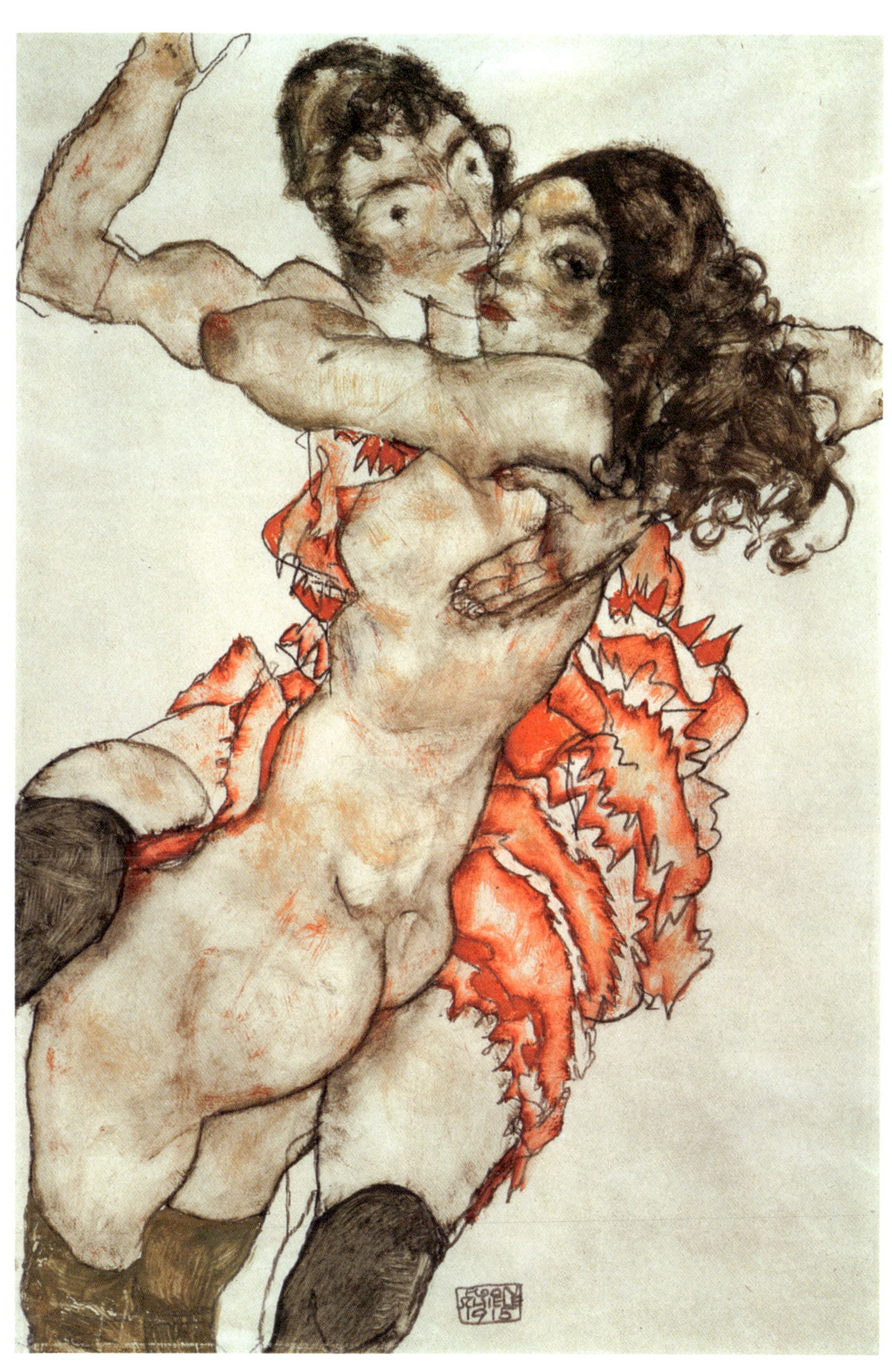

Egon Schiele
Two Women, 1915
Gouache, watercolour and pencil on paper, 48.5 × 32.7 cm
Private collection

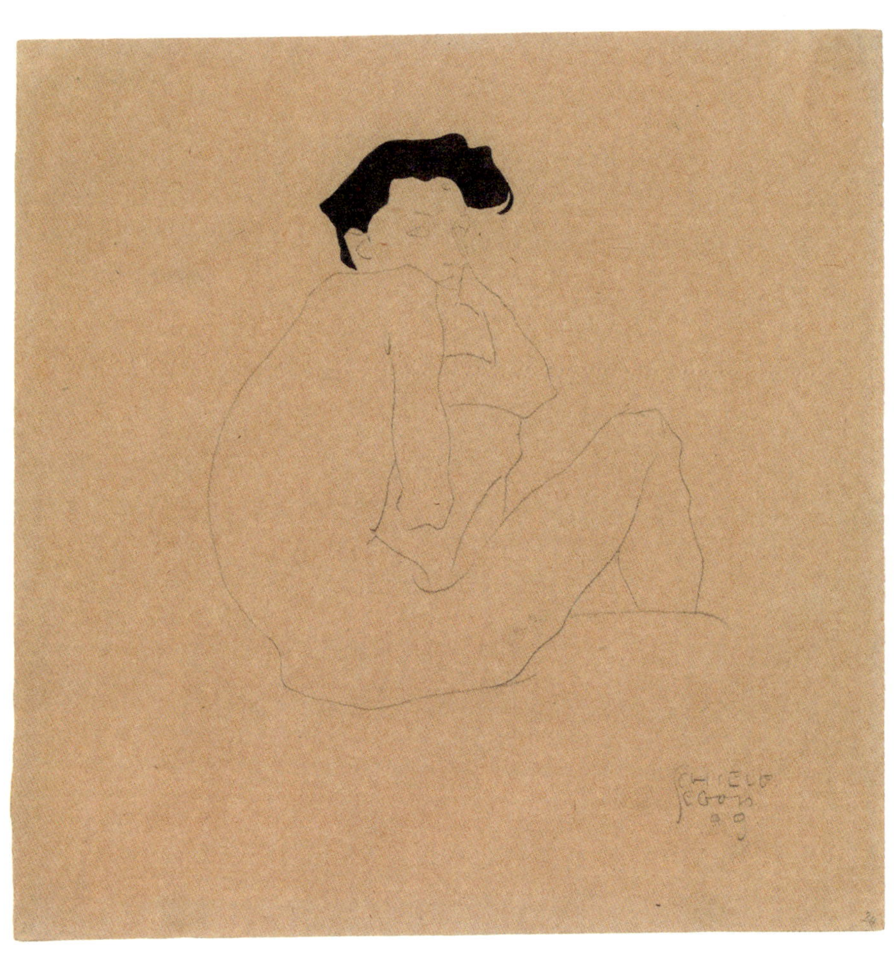

Egon Schiele
Seated Male Nude (Self-Portrait), 1909
Indian ink and pencil on paper, 32 × 31.8 cm
International Modern Art Foundation Belgium

fact that no one can define the word 'beautiful'. Filling one's home exclusively with aesthetically pleasing works is subject to the judgement of beauty, which changes over time. And buying art in the expectation that it will still be what people will want in the future can turn out badly after a few years when the taste judgement of buyers undergoes a drastic change. Any judgement of taste must be based on reason: only then does art emerge. Those who view contemporary art from a visionary angle and place modern art in its historical timeline will understand the grandeur of art. This capital-A Art inscribes itself in history, while those things that were merely deemed beautiful have no chance of making it on to the eternal artistic stage. Egon Schiele broke with the Romantic style of his time and, for all that he is highly regarded nowadays, his provocative art landed him in prison in 1912 at the age of twenty-two. Art lovers, by contrast, understand the importance of art like this with reference to its origins. Schiele's work must be considered in context. Only then does the special power of his autonomy emerge – a genuine gift within the artistic poverty of his time. He brought a reality that is not a lie, but a truth. Great artists distance themselves from what is considered beautiful, from what seduces the public, and struggle – sometimes at risk of their very existence – to confront and reject everything that has been achieved before. Artists like this, who extricate themselves from tradition, strive to be reborn at the new beginning. They are looking for a new life with new challenges. In modern art, therefore, the emergence of the *new sense of beauty* entails a new path that can only be found in the absolute authenticity of the work of art itself. Consequently, when contemporary art is linked to the old idea of beauty, it soon ends up as *a single great bubble*.

Andy Warhol (1928–1987) fought against society's conventions in his own eccentric and theatrical way, making him a symbol of the new American lifestyle of the 1960s. He utterly ignored what had been commonplace in painting for centuries, preferring instead to produce like a machine and refusing to follow the conventions of painting. Warhol also rejected the dichotomy between high and low culture and proved that there was barely any difference between a soup can and a queen. When it comes to consuming, there is little distinction between rich and poor Americans: they are influenced by the same advertising and watch the same Hollywood movies. Warhol's iconography presents us with American buildings, newspaper photos, Brillo boxes and Campbell's Soup as everyday fare, but also series of portraits and skulls and much more besides – iconic registrations from the trendy 1960s. His Pop Art was the most marginalized art ever, devoid of emotion. The process by which Warhol created his art occurred without direct human physical input. His chosen subject matter led to a void, which was then reincarnated as a new object that in turn became art – a kind of vampirism. Warhol was the first mass communicator and was

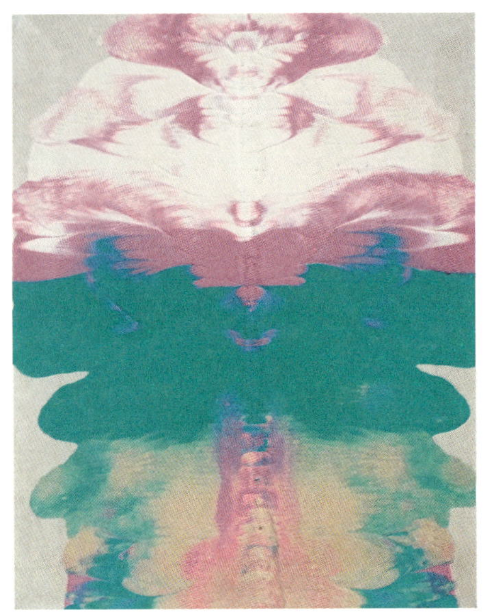

revolutionary with his *concept of emptiness*, the absence of any content. He broke with all the painting techniques used in the art world up to that point. Warhol created from his brain, barely employing his hands at all, and his silkscreen printing technique was diametrically opposed to the brush strokes of the revolutionary avant-garde of his time.

Beauty in art is very changeable: each new generation has its own judgement of taste. One constantly follows another, and every generation lives in a new time, in a new context, in which new subcultures develop in turn. Those who buy art later in life and/or without experience, are often guided by their own judgement of beauty, only to realize all too quickly that their choices are very much of their time and rapidly lose their resale value. People buy according to their old habits. Things that are new or unusual strike them as ugly, even if that is what the latest generations are holding out. Conversely, what the older generation finds beautiful is opposite to the taste judgement of those who will shape the future. Past beauty stands for tranquillity; it functions like wallpaper and, unlike anarchistic productions, does not impose a dialogue about art. It is a stagnating beauty. Art that lacks the autonomous power derived from a historic new beginning is far from beautiful. But an artistic expression that caused a stir in the past retains that in its genes and derives its raison d'être from it. Recognition of this fact sets viewers on a train of thought that also calls them to reflect on the new importance of our contemporary art. A work of art bought purely because of its beauty will swiftly become obsolete. Art that is ahead of its time requires an effort on the viewer's part, but at the same time will continue to fascinate for many generations to come. Contemporary art thus invites us to raise our *mental and financial pain threshold*: to learn to see what we have previously rejected, even if its purchase value will not be easy to overcome. The effort to understand contemporary art is a fascinating recipe that also teaches you how to look at art within a universal, historical context.

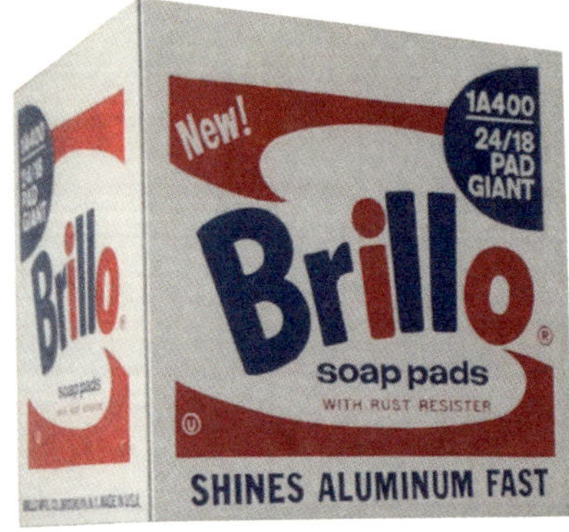

Andy Warhol
Rorschach, 1984
Acrylic paint on canvas, 50 × 40 cm
International Modern Art Foundation Belgium

Andy Warhol
Brillo Box (Stockholm type), 1964/68
Silkscreen ink on chipboard, 44 × 44 × 36 cm
International Modern Art Foundation Belgium

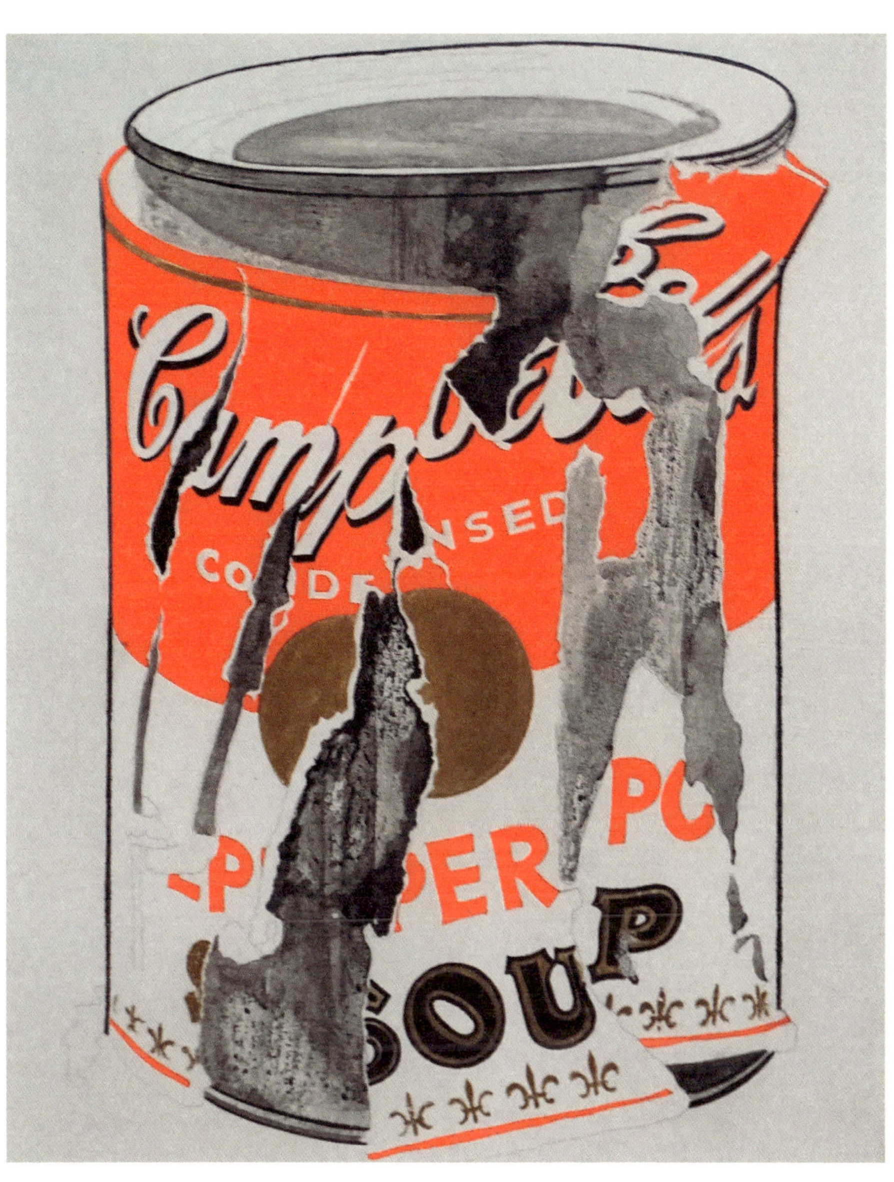

Andy Warhol
Small Torn Campbell's Soup Can (Pepper Pot), 1962
Casein, gilding and graphite on canvas, 50.8 × 40.6 cm
Los Angeles, The Broad

Art is rarely easy to understand, but it offers a pleasure that is forward-looking and overwhelming.

All the same, there are several figures in contemporary art who have kept the bubble inflating. In their artistic message, created within the new context in which the world is evolving, they have made kitsch and bad taste artistically acceptable. In 1988, Jeff Koons (b. 1955) employed a visual language in which religious idols gave way to popular icons from mass culture. He depicted a series of kitsch embraces in porcelain and polychrome wooden sculptures. With figures like Michael Jackson and his chimpanzee Bubbles, the stuffed toy Popples, Buster Keaton and the Pink Panther, Jeff Koons brought the kitsch of mass production into the art world, elevating it to the level of art. His marriage to porn star La Cicciolina swiftly became part of his creative practice too. The explicit photographs and sculptures of himself and his wife making love courted controversy, from which Koons defended himself through an artistic innocence. He alluded to human biology, to sexuality between lovers and to the survival of the human species. His photos and sculptures rendered acceptable in this way, he took his truth and rode it to star status. Koons goaded good taste, with each of his shows oscillating between cheap and cynical popular entertainment and jubilant revelation. The absolute authenticity of his art ought to have triggered a new and universal sense of beauty, yet for the public it came as a shock. It was marvellous to witness how accurately Koons hit his target and succeeded in astonishing the art world with his work.

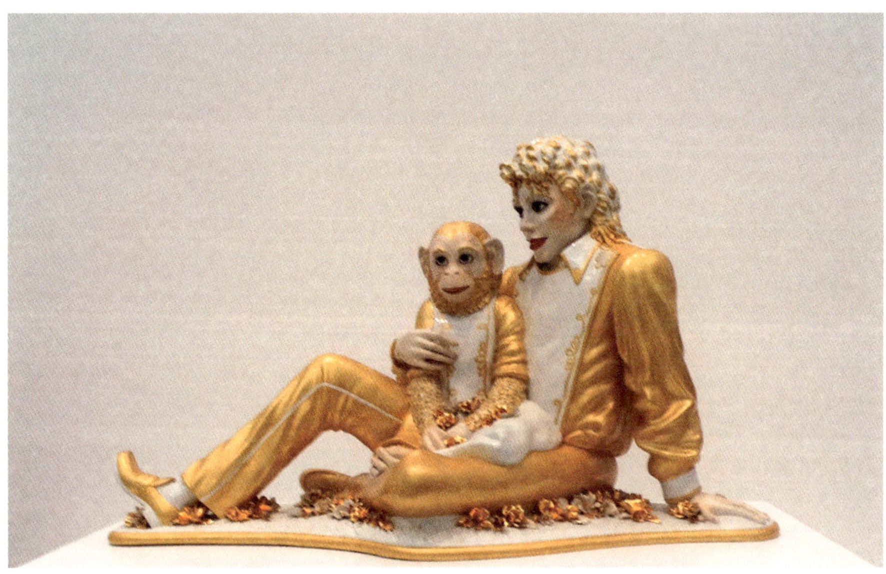

Jeff Koons
Michael Jackson & Bubbles, 1988–89
Porcelain, 106.7 × 179.1 × 82.6 cm
San Francisco Museum of Modern Art

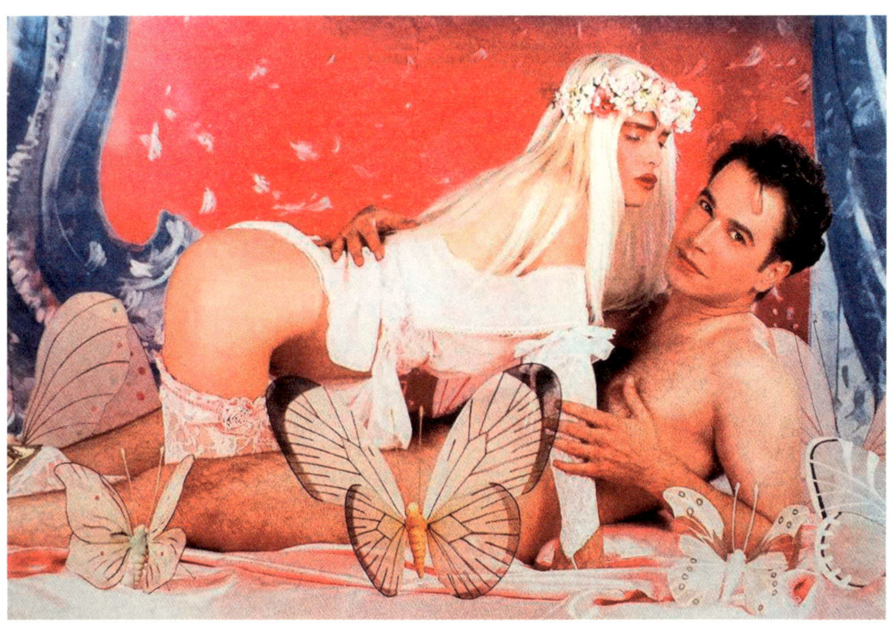

Koons' *kalliphobia* (*kallos* meaning beauty and *phobos* fear) turns his work against the notion of beauty that art has appropriated for itself since the Renaissance. Alongside art's anarchistic streak, a similar 'kalliphobia' spread like an epidemic across avant-garde circles in the early twentieth century. The term was coined by the American art critic and philosopher Arthur Danto (1924–2013), who defined it as fear of the standard aesthetic condition that acts as a mollifying lowest common denominator and is reflected in everything as an existential precondition. The avant-garde art world opposed what the mass of the people perceived to be beautiful, something that was not recognized in the assessment of art. The philosophy of art studies how artists create a work, how the public interacts with it, and the subjective and sensory and emotional values of beauty and taste. It examines how our minds judge what we see, read or listen to within the aesthetic rules of art we have had imposed upon us. Are we experiencing pleasure in what we see or are we adhering to an imposed value judgement? Does the aesthetic experience of art affect our state of mind and influence the question of 'What is art?' Is aesthetics merely a *critical reflection* on what we see, and ought we not then to be wary of the logical conclusion that the existence of art is illuminated merely by the momentum of the artist's own existence? A copy of an earlier style, no matter how accomplished, is never art. Does this imply that the importance of the art in question is extremely short-lived and

Jeff Koons
Made in Heaven, 1989
Oil inks on canvas, 243.3 × 365.8 cm
Private collection

good only for historical accumulation? And will the answer to every question about art hence be left unanswered forever?

OPTICAL TRUTH

A shockwave ran through the art world around 1826 when the Frenchman Nicéphore Niépce (1765–1833) took the first permanently fixed photograph. His brainchild triggered a profound renewal in art. The exposure to light in a camera obscura of a plate coated with photosensitive material resulted in the first photographic city views and landscapes. The artistic imitation that had historically dominated painting and sculpture took a radically new turn in response to Niépce's invention. In 1858, the French author Nadar (1820–1910) shot the first aerial photograph, before going on in the years that followed to float above Paris and other cities in his hot-air balloon taking pictures more or less at random. His insouciance would, however, be short-lived: four years later, the French artist Honoré Daumier (1808–1879) drew a cartoon featuring Nadar's aerial exploits, which he captioned *Nadar élevant la Photographie à la hauteur de l'Art* (Nadar Elevating Photography to the Height of Art). Its publication caused a furore in the art world. The innocent aerial snapshots referred to in the 1862 cartoon marked the beginning of modern art. Daumier's tongue-in-cheek caption was taken literally: photography had abruptly achieved an equal (if not higher) status to painting. An affronted art world was faced with a new beginning across the board. The cartoon implied that there was no longer any place for imitation in the definition of art. Photography – followed not long after by moving film – possessed the ability to create extremely true-to-life images, obliging art to seek new directions. So it was that Nicéphore Niépce, the great hero of photography, inscribed himself at the origin of an important change that heralded the beginning of modern art. It gradually dawned on people that photography could express certain things, with which painting consequently no longer had to concern itself – it seemed crazy to paint what the lens could now capture instantly. Photography emerged at precisely the right time to liberate painting from imposed forms and subject matter. The shock delivered by Niépce encouraged real artists to engage in a profound self-examination.

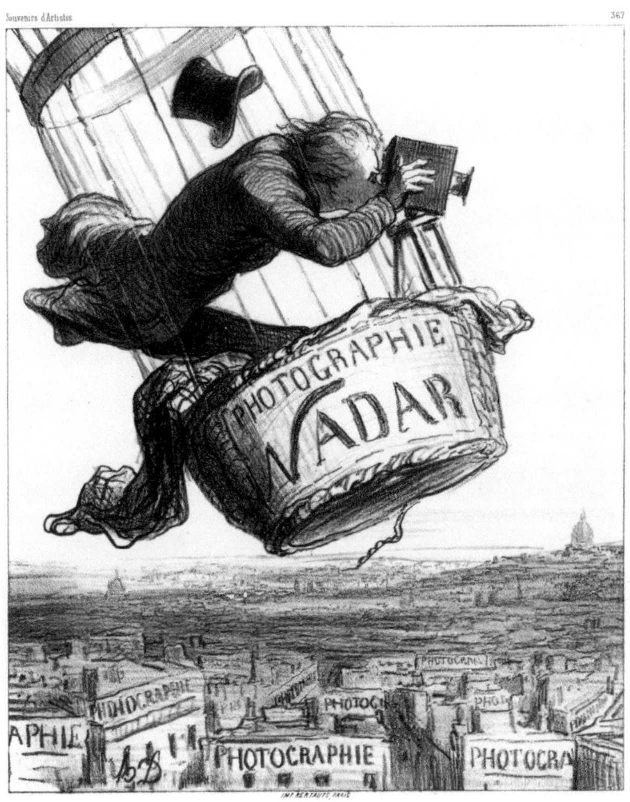

NADAR, élevant la Photographie à la hauteur de l'Art

Henceforward, photography had subjects of its own, enabling artists to begin experimenting. Obsolete ideas and outmoded definitions were abandoned in both sculpture and painting and it now fell to artists to establish new ideas in their place. Artists regained their freedom, triggering fresh stylistic revolutions that would go on to write modern art history.

Portrait painters were the first to feel the repercussions of the new medium. They noticed, for instance, that the expression of a person portrayed in a photograph was completely different to that of a sitter in a painting. It came as a shock to realize that no painter was able to render their human observation in as sensory a manner as a photograph did. Artists revert to certain stereotypes when creating a portrait, something that the camera does entirely differently. Today's cameras can capture up to sixty or so different images in the space of a second – a fragmentary gaze that

Honoré Daumier
Nadar Elevating Photography to the Height of Art, 1862
Lithograph, 33.7 × 24.8 cm
New York, Brooklyn Museum

is not natural to human beings and which they are even less capable of capturing in a painted canvas. No artist could ever recall with such precision what they have seen and then set it down with equal accuracy using a given technique. The human eye is limited, in other words, with the result that human beings create their own sensory reality via a process of thought – one that differs from objective reality. The advent of photography thus confronted the experimenting artist and the art world with 'a new beginning'. It was time for modern portrait painters to apply themselves to what photography could *not* do: from now on, they would paint their models through their personal perception. They used their brushes to depict the sitter's character, adding intellectual value to their artistic expression. Henceforth, painters and sculptors based their portraits on what they thought about the person being portrayed, rather than simply on what they saw. The truth-to-life that had defined the beauty of the portrait was found to be a mirage and duly vanished. A new truth emerged through the artist's imagination, and the objective representation of reality that had typified a now obsolete portraiture faded away.

Photography did, however, become an important tool for painters of horses, who were now able to study a galloping horse properly before painting it. Photographs offered more than the human eye can see, allowing the quadruped's precise movement to be captured and reproduced. More effectively, at any rate, than the stiff-legged springboks we find in aquatints of racehorses by Charles Hunt (1803–1877). Photography robbed painting of the aspiration to perfect imitation that had dominated it for centuries. Nothing sought any longer to live up to the requirements of earlier artistic creations. Since the rise of photography, established artists concerned themselves exclusively with the intellectual context of the art of their time, leaving stereotypical ideals of beauty bereft of any further interest. This minor history of photography, which played out within the larger sweep of history, was thanks to the inventor Nicéphore Niépce from Saint-Loup-de-Varennes. It was radical in the extreme and would shape the entire course of art history.

A key factor in the structure of *The Execution of Maximilian* (1868–1869), Edouard Manet's indictment of the French emperor, was that photography was banned from recording the event. The fact that there were no photographs to show precisely how the execution played out makes the work even more exceptional. Manet had to reconstruct the incident from newspaper reports and hearsay. The public's understanding of what had happened shifted over time, which prompted the artist to paint the subject several times, adjusting it on each successive occasion. Several works on the theme were found in Manet's studio after his death. In his first attempt, the artist painted a squad of Mexican guerrillas in sombreros. These were subsequently replaced by regular Mexican soldiers in uniform. Manet's penultimate

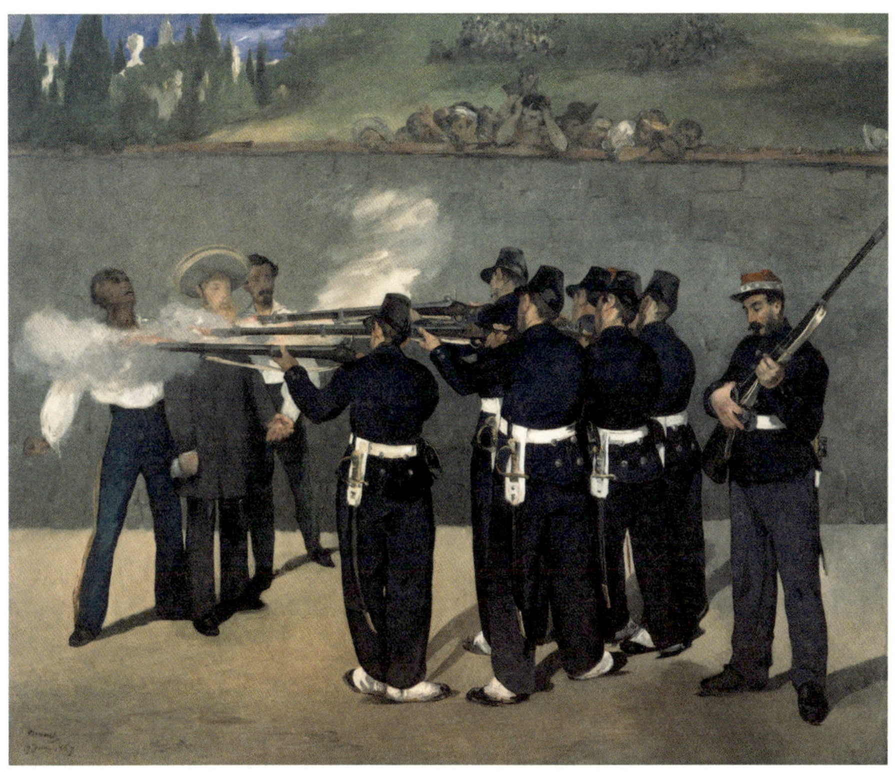

painting presents an anarchistic picture of a firing squad wearing French uniforms to place the blame on those ultimately responsible for Maximilian's execution. In the fifth and final painting, the French soldiers actually fire the fatal shots. The liberal-minded artist and political opponent of Napoleon III did not finish his first version of the execution. He continually changed his mind and it was only the last, most anarchistic version of the theme that he completed, affirming its truth. In this final iteration, the artist placed the features of Napoleon III on the soldier on the right, who will fire the last shot. Drawing on the power of his imagination, Edouard Manet created an image that goes beyond a naturalistic representation and is free of any imitation of reality. Manet's critical rendering of the execution placed him on the map as an artist. His new mode of imagination/representation turned the art world upside down and achieved the biggest and most important caesura in painting. Perfect imitation and aesthetic correctness had been the absolute standards of beauty throughout previous centuries, right back to the Italian Renaissance and Giotto's *Ognissanti Madonna*. Monet the anarchist taught us the power of art in exposing lies.

Edouard Manet
The Execution of Emperor Maximilian, 1868–69
Oil on canvas, 252 × 302 cm
Kunsthalle Mannheim

It was around this same time that Gustave Courbet (1819–1877) painted a work that was highly realistic, but which the Frenchman knew would shock the public, precisely because of that realism. The *Origin of the World* (1866) is a small canvas that simply depicts a vulva. It is a naturalistic, rather affectless painting that describes the female genitals with almost anatomical precision. So confrontational was the work that it was hidden away for over a century, before finally ending up in the Musée d'Orsay in 1995. Courbet was a pioneer who had already produced groundbreaking work, yet this form of realism was new and marked the beginning of absolute freedom in art.

He painted the woman's torso in close-up, with the vulva in the centre between her thighs and a perspective view of the curve of her stomach and one of her breasts. The depiction of pubic hair was also highly unusual in painting. Through this work, the artist was able to taunt the establishment, while doing no more than to depict an explicit reality. We might ask whether Courbet's intention was indeed to shock the viewer, or whether he painted the canvas purely out of a sense of realism, albeit taking a subject that was very unusual in art. Would the work have been seen as equally offensive, for instance, if Courbet had not depicted the genitals so realistically? Would viewers then have been put off the painting by its lack of realism, or would the painter's aesthetic interpretation have charmed them? Can we still talk of a shock if the viewer unconsciously collaborates with the painter's aesthetic goal and – as if through the eyes of the painter himself – pursues a similarly corrected realism? If so, does the antagonist not then become the protagonist, who only survives within the story of art by virtue of the innovative idea? On the cusp of a modern art that is averse to any sense of realism, Gustave Courbet proved with *The Origin of the World* that realism itself can raise questions.

The notion of 'artistic autonomy' was unknown prior to the end of the eighteenth century. Artists were not yet regarded as gods: they had not yet become the creator of a universe filled with their own personal laws and rules. A rigid society continued to be dominated by immutable opinions. All the same, every three generations or so a need arose for something new. Authority evolved and contemporary art became more accepted. Hence the reason that artists in the nineteenth century were able to seize the opportunity to alert their society to its flaws. They held up a critical mirror and offered fresh ideas to stimulate the further development of society itself. Where their criticism was misunderstood, their art was dismissed as a worthless joke. But those aspects to which the powers-that-be did prove receptive went on in turn to enrich society. The open gaze that artists imposed on society also brought art closer to the people. If the public would not come to art, art could still influence the public. It played a similar role in that regard to the

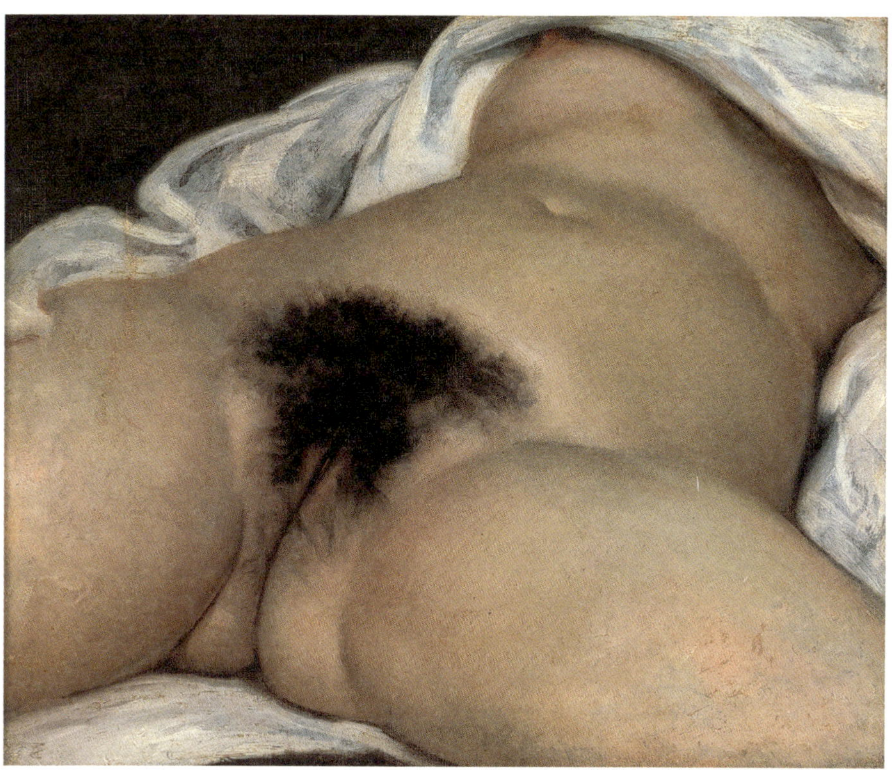

court jester – allowed greater freedom of speech than the average citizen. Avant-garde artists like Francisco de Goya, Edouard Manet and Eugène Delacroix likewise raged against society through their artistic resistance to previous generations. In the course of the rebellion against academicism, artists rubbed shoulders with elite circles, whose conscience they helped extricate from the laws of the conditioned community. Art wormed its way innocently into the crowd, questioning boundaries and breaking through the stagnation of its time. It successfully challenged an entire political establishment. This evolution created space for social development and for the personal development of engaged individuals.

There is no obligation to pursue beauty when collecting modern and contemporary art: even bad taste can be artistically acceptable. Pursuing beauty seems like a safe option, but art is much more about the artist's inner message. If collectors fail to distinguish true art from the rest, it might because they prefer to align themselves with a group. And group inertia invariably means that innovation is lost. Their shared approval of a work is generally based on a pre-digested aesthetic

Gustave Courbet
The Origin of the World, 1866
Oil on canvas, 46.3 × 55.4 cm
Paris, Musée d'Orsay

judgement, which is not what makes a masterpiece. For their part, artists do not have golden rules and what groups of viewers think they are discovering swiftly turns out to be superficial and bland. At the same time, there is nothing unusual about a creative person and their ego wanting to see their work hanging in a museum. Yet such a destination surely represents the beginning of an uncritical, deathly silence around that same creation? Museum acquisitions, imposed by the judgement of a single generation, are frequently doomed to end up as *generation art* in these institutional funeral homes. Art can swiftly become outmoded because of the taste of a particular generation. Conversely, it can actually benefit when its own generation judges and condemns it. Surely collectors and museums should learn from this? How can you continue to justify purchasing an object in the name of art, without crossing the mental and financial pain threshold? Contemporary art needs museums that create space to organize and actualize our present and do so with a visionary eye. Museums exist to teach us how to look at art in the spirit of our times, not simply to nurture art forever until it dies. The Uffizi in Florence has Giotto's *Ognissanti Madonna* and the Musée d'Orsay in Paris has Gustave Courbet's *Origin of the World* – two controversial icons in the history of our art. They represent the beginning of fourteenth-century aesthetics and that of nineteenth-century free-thinking in modern art, and they are works that make us think too. Museums have been prepared to include contemporary art in their collections in recent decades, although this tends to occur far too soon and irreversibly. Artists should be left to enjoy the mental freedom of first allowing their work to develop fully in their studios. Incorporating art in a collection too early while a potentially much more fascinating oeuvre is still developing constrains the true artist.

Given this new mentality in contemporary art, a danger of a dissection, an unravelling in search of meaning, constantly threatens art today. The studio is the place where artists' ideas mature – it should be the artistic individual who takes the lead, not the museum. Placing too much importance on a young artist too soon works like a perfume: if the public succumbs passionately to its allure, it sells not only itself short but also the artist, who has a need for total freedom. Measuring or qualifying an artist's talent might help mitigate the current collective focus for a particular icon – the 'winner-takes-all' mentality – so that he or she does not come to be regarded too soon as a phenomenon, destined all too often to achieve only short-lived success. The twenty-first century and all the opportunities it has offered for manipulation has dealt the art world a serious slap in the face. There is a danger that museum directors and curators will stop seeking out good artists themselves: who is not seduced by the galleries that dominate the art market with their hyped-up artists? Price-setting by high-profile auctions leaves seekers after art blind and half-crazed. In this way, the art trade creates a terrain that borders on the incestuous. Perhaps museums ought just to place a specific price tag on each work?

Social, economic and technological mechanisms allow a constant search for shared knowledge and taste. The advent of the internet and social media means that winners are winning more and even faster than ever, and that they are sufficiently armed nowadays against the scorn of the masses. These seductive techniques prey on a great many susceptible art lovers, who pursue their artistic pleasure all too docilely and thoughtlessly. Commercial art and society are thus readily connected by money, while the world of real art remains uncomfortable about it. The question arises as to whether *generation art* of this kind can still be enjoyed, when the artistic judgement is imposed by a self-appointed online intelligentsia. The power of social networks in their entirety amounts to no more than a sad, fake freedom. Art is knowledge, but those who seek it are, unfortunately, seduced and misled by the new media. If social media considers its art to be the new reality, then there is no more art. Which means in turn that we will miss the true geniuses, who are only recognized when the public vilifies them. Meanwhile, spectators themselves are bound by laws and rules that invisibly brainwash them. So even if art still has to be 'beautiful', the object always comes first, following which the viewer passes judgement on it according to fossilized standards of beauty. It is always the importance of the object itself that first determines the meaning of the word 'art'. Surely this art itself should be allowed to continue its long journey before any attempt is made to understand and protect it?

ART IS, BECAUSE IT HAS BECOME SO

Viewers derive their pursuit of meaning in an artistic creation from the importance of art. Such creations offer pleasure, and those who look at them do not have to justify what they see or wish to see. Anyone who is open to what can be seen when viewing a work that has never been seen or described before grants what they see the freedom of existence. This attitude represents the evolution of the one who is beholding, the evolution of the self. Receptivity – aside from reading or understanding a message – completes the act of looking. It heightens the feeling of what one sees. Art is a world entire, and it helps us to feel and to understand what is around us. This is what we learn from our youngest children, when they innocently describe what they see in a sculpture or painting. Art is a unity of meaningful representations or forms that live in a world of their own: a pictorial universe that is not the same as concrete reality, but which invites you to get to know and to question yourself. The new era led artists to this new thinking. Modern artists destroyed what was considered beautiful and sought a fresh way to express themselves through art. No further attempt was made to build on the old ideal of beauty. This was the point at which artists aspired to create 'absolute art' with their new achievements. The artwork became something different for the artist's soul: no longer subservient to the urge for pure material provocation. The aesthetic judgement of beauty ceased to be important. Art now stood for 'the absolute moment of clarity' and the work of art was granted a pardon once again.

There were no longer any rules in art in the twentieth century, so that we ceased to be impressed more by a perfectly finished artwork than by a more rough-and-ready piece. Aesthetic beauty has had its day, and those who admire art purely for its importance no longer seek it through an aesthetic value. The concept of a work of art is associated with the genius of its maker, opening the viewer to the artist's entirely new ideas. Reflection on art is thus situated in the way an idea is embodied, making the artist the creator of meaning rather than just that of an expected beauty. Art that is merely beautiful and perfect is clearly diminishing in importance, precisely because nothing can be expressed through sheer beauty. If a work of art contains a meaning that appeals because of its authenticity, it possesses genuine scope, a power that renders art meaningful. So long as these works of art are talked about, we will continue to think about them and their existence will serve a purpose.

An artwork is a composition consisting of an organized system of colours, planes and lines. To find more than a void in this interplay of forms, a vocabulary is needed to formulate the expression of the work. A work of art is originally 'empty', in fact. Only when a human being approaches it is it enriched by the interpretative power of the word. The art lover animates it, following which the work comes to life, its existence is acknowledged and it becomes an energized object. In 1953, the French philosopher Mikel Dufrenne (1910–1995) wrote *Phénoménologie de l'expérience esthétique*, in which he argued that art is a quasi-subject, since through its communicative authority the thing – the object – emerges from a hidden existence to become almost a subject. It is precisely because of this communicative character that art gains its voice, because from a previously unknown object, it has become a meaningful quasi-subject. The quasi-subject is more than just a thing, since it arises in a shared world – the world of the beholder and the world of the thing itself – shaped by the one who gave it expression. It is through this power that a culture-object lives and a conscious, shared narrative emerges. Thanks to the judgement of the true patron, the work of art will take its place in the art world separately from its sensory qualities. It is here that the concept of the artwork lies and from here that interpretations arise that become public. Those who interpret demonstrate a vision and can invite the public to think with them more deeply. It is precisely through this confrontation that art clearly and justifiably lives beyond its existence, in dialogue with the time in which the artwork is located.

The 'subject against object' idea in Mikel Dufrenne's philosophy is interesting today when applied to Chinese culture. Towards the end of the twentieth century, traditional Chinese art was derailed and a sudden 'subject against object' movement arose for the first time among artists themselves. In a country where political pressure prevented citizens from developing as individuals, a sense of obligatory equality long held sway. Communism obliged citizens to behave like objects: they had no control nor any possibility for developing their own personality. Chinese citizens had to regard themselves as objects and to behave accordingly, no more than that. But this was not to last. In 1989, Beijing witnessed the Tiananmen Square protests, in which around a million students and citizens resisted the authorities. This mass opposition to the Communist Party culminated in a bloodbath on Tiananmen Square, with thousands losing their lives. In the aftermath, Chinese people no longer behaved like objects without a say, and dissident artists became active internationally. Modern art that previously aped the work of earlier Western artists, was no more. Artists who had pursued pure beauty in response to an imposed idea, like an uncritical object, now became a quasi-subject. They embarked on an anarchistic struggle and their work likewise became a quasi-subject. Those who used their talent to challenge the lies of the state created a new truth. Henceforward, Chinese art enjoyed a global importance. We refer in art history to 'the third Mecca', which offered a new art at the beginning of the twenty-first century within an emerging economic power. This Chinese School succeeded the American School, which had in turn displaced the Ecole de Paris.

Freedom enables human beings to become individuals, capable of creating art. Sadly, after thirty years, Chinese dissident art has once more been restricted; Hong Kong has come under Chinese control following the introduction in 2022 of the National Security Law, and the gates to understanding by the free West have been closed again to any genuine artist. Art as a quasi-subject was short-lived and, for their part, artists themselves have been obliged once more to view and conduct themselves as objects. *The Execution of Christ* (2009) by the Gao Brothers (b. 1956 and 1962), for instance, is a monumental example of dissident art that would be impossible to exhibit in today's China under Xi Jingping. The work recalls the Mao regime and stands for critical thinking and so, like the protest in Tiananmen Square, is considered transgressive.

Ai Weiwei (b. 1957) too has denounced the Maoist indoctrination that has undermined his country. His pointed criticism has the power to shock and he uses art to expose China's underlying reality and in doing so to improve the lives of the Chinese people. It is through this confrontation that he delivers his critique and tries to dislodge people from outmoded ways of thinking. There is a danger in Europe too that people will be stifled in their creative power and unable to continue expressing their anarchistic message.

Composers need musicians to perform their creation to an audience. It takes a long time to write a symphony and even longer before it can be fully performed and heard. Visual art, by contrast, has an immediate resonance and is never dependent on who reads, publishes or performs it. What you create with your hands is immediately realized in life, it is concrete and hence unmistakable. Labelling it as 'art' thus demands a reaction. The number of people looking at art today is lower than the number of artworks being looked at. The constant quest for art has resulted in a long procession of works that can only diminish the viewer's concentration. Multiplying the viewing experience diminishes its exceptional nature. Consequently, anyone who observes this procession uncritically leaves themselves dependent on the transient. By constantly cherishing new expectations, they demonstrate that they do

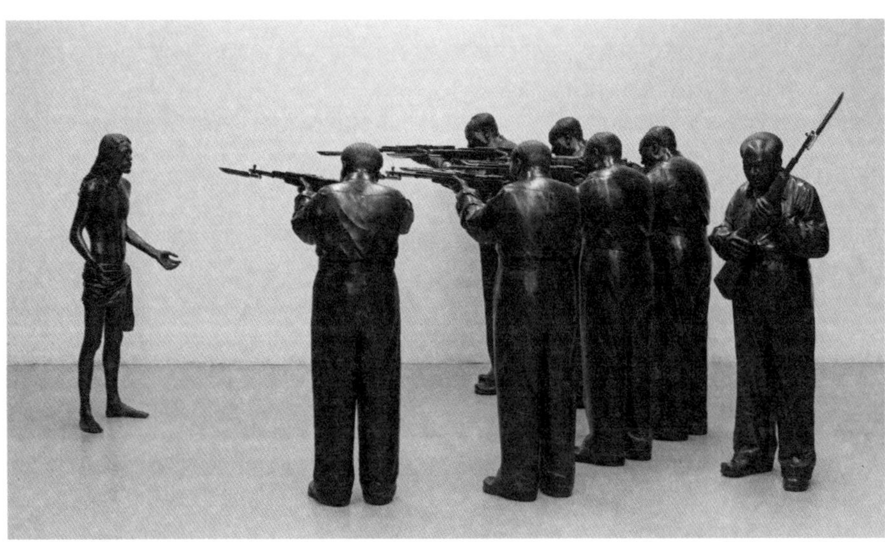

Gao Brothers
The Execution of Christ, 2009
Bronze, life-size
International Modern Art Foundation Belgium

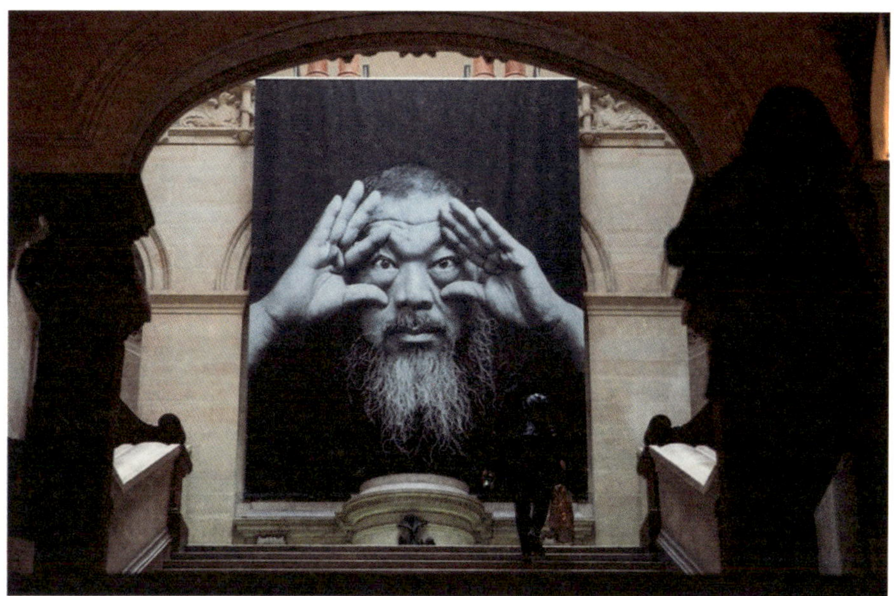

not actually wish to experience art, even though deep observation is precisely what is important. Contemporary art requires more than mere viewing of its form. As a result of this habituation, born of excess, a mass accumulation is occurring of objects masquerading as art. Admiring this kind of imitation reduces it to a decorative existence entirely lacking in autonomy, a state of artistic stagnation. An artist who goes in search of purity, by contrast, stands at the beginning of an end – the necessary end point, which also has to be seen as a necessary new starting point.

The French artist Jean Rustin (1928–2013) resolutely paints humanity in all its ugliness. His duty as a painter leads him to opt consciously for this new visual language, with which he paints disconcerting nudes, brilliantly yet at once crudely and cynically. The exposed genitals, often in the context of a sexual act, are anything but erotic or beautiful. Viewers are confronted with themselves, as it were, an image they would rather avoid. The artist is driven by compassion, as if his works represented our naked truth. He does not create ideal images of the female or male nude, but observes the human ageing process and makes no attempt to produce pretty pictures. With painful precision and without flinching at decay, he holds up an oversized mirror to us of a nakedness that is ugly. His figures are situated in a minimalist space, which does not distract the viewer from the subject. Rustin creates tender and compassionate images of vulnerability and physical deterioration.

Ai Weiwei, Venice, 2017

The earlier judgement of beauty is done with and has given way to a new beginning with an uncertain new idea. Contemporary art is no longer subject to laws, and the desire for the aesthetic beauty of the past has faded away. Lawless contemporary art is spontaneously and imprecisely free. Everything now is clear and bright. There are no longer any rules for understanding the complexity of art, only the necessary brainpower to recognize its brilliant simplicity. A persistent philosophical thinking relegates all previous conceptions to a secondary level and probes the evolution of art. While that exploration is going on, a fresh truth emerges. Nothing, then, is determinative, not even an art movement. Nothing is complete, but rather incomplete, uncertain and merely contingent. Over time, a new truth will always delineate itself through new frontiers, with the power and ability to expand. A new context will thus gradually emerge, in which 'the new everything' will be found. This is linked in turn with a number of philosophical notions, the existence of which is accepted, pointing the way once again to innovative art. Art is as it is because it has become so. Seeking the meaning of art and thinking about what it has become proves the essence of its existence. It is important to understand first how art became what it is.

It never occurred to Pablo Picasso to make a statue in marble: he thought the stone was boring; it did nothing to inspire him. The artist preferred to capture something by seeing a form in a material that was within reach. He detected forms like this in rough stones, bones, walls and pieces of wood. His sculptures were created from scrap materials or he discovered them in nature. Behind the famous artist, then, was a man who studied things in depth. He was completely absorbed in what he saw and his fervent curiosity gave rise to a strong ability to concentrate, the likely key to his talent. He filed away everything mentally – names, words, faces, things – and was extraordinarily permeated by everything he saw. It was this concentration that enabled him to make use of all the forms from reality at any time. Once he had seen them, they remained etched in his memory forever. He had only to touch his canvas with the tip of his brush to spontaneously conjure up the object as a new reality.

Picasso collected all sorts of things that others threw away. Jean Cocteau called him 'the king of the rag-pickers'. His love of simple things and discarded materials filled his head with ideas. But his jacket pockets were also stuffed full and occasionally ripped because of all the 'knickknacks' he stowed in them. His hands were constantly reaching for discarded objects, in which his eyes detected bison, monsters or human heads. For instance, Picasso designed an especially accomplished collage for the cover of the first issue of *Minotaure*, a Surrealist-oriented magazine founded in Paris by Albert Skira and Tériade. It appeared on 25 May 1933. The model for the cover was made of corrugated card fixed to a wooden board with

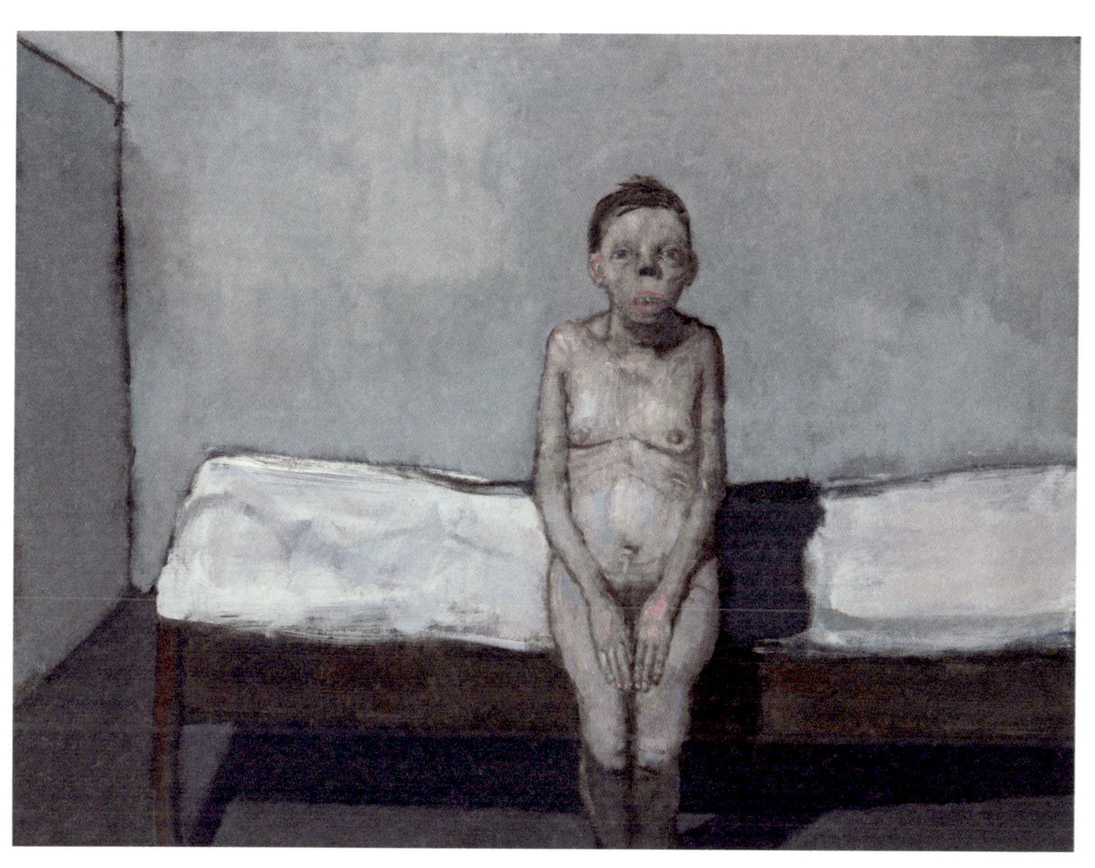

Jean Rustin
Woman Sitting on Bed, 1996
Oil on canvas, 98 × 130 cm
International Modern Art Foundation Belgium

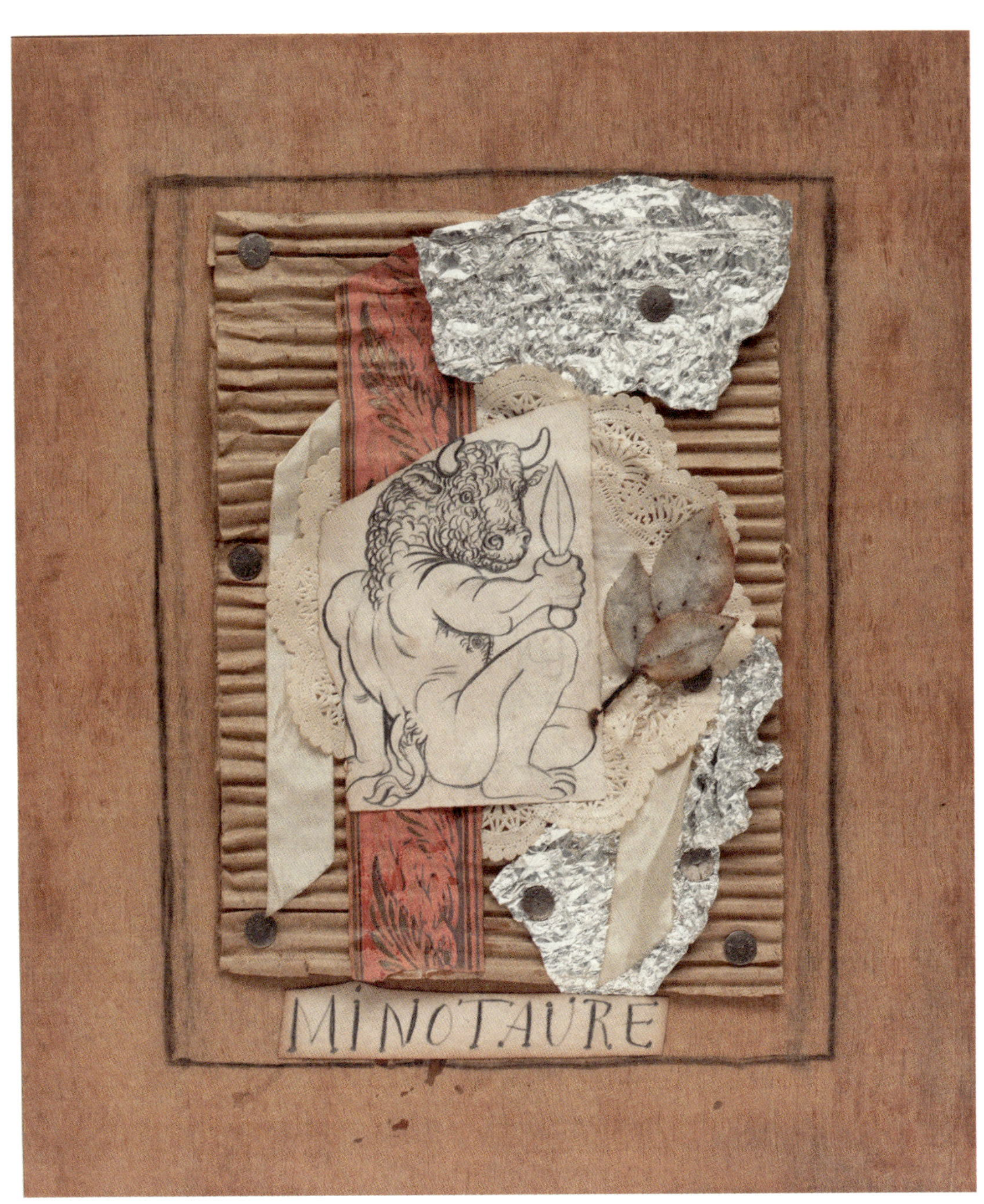

Pablo Picasso
Model for the cover of the art magazine *Minotaure*, 1933
Assemblage, mixed media, 48.5 × 41 cm
New York, MoMA

thumb tacks. A burin engraving of a minotaur was mounted on to this, surrounded by ribbons, silver paper and pieces of fabric from an old hat belonging to Picasso's first wife, Olga Khokhlova. His work might have had a whiff of heresy, but there are no doctrines in modern art. He was guided by his capacity to think rather than by the taste and collective judgement of a populace out to consume. The true artist has no need to be judged anyway. Misunderstanding by the general public is followed by the encounter with a true art lover.

The inner energy of the artist is like a concentrated drop of transparent medication that dissolves invisibly in a glass of water. The glass looks exactly like any other, yet the effect of its contents will be totally different. The concentrated droplet functions like the fuse to a gunpowder keg. This is also how the work of Jean-Michel Basquiat (1960–1988) came to be born, an artist who was himself a vessel overflowing with urges. His creations were fuelled by the racist society in which he grew up as a Black American and his life was shaped by the urge to use his artistic fantasies to criticize power structures and social inequality. Basquiat lived in New York, where he was known for a social engagement expressed through graffiti and street art. He hit the bullseye: his work drew attention, though it was criticized too, and went on to establish a place for itself in the history of art. After centuries of racism in US society, African-American art developed its own visual language. It was a new beginning and the context in which Basquiat's artistic personality developed. With his aggressive texts and expressive imagery, he offered painting from an existing yet unknown culture. A voice crying out to demand its rights in an ignorant environment. The young Black artist expressed himself as the earliest African-American painter. He began with street art, was invited by the gallery owner Annina Nosei to use her basement as a studio, and ended up at the very heart of modern American art history. There was more to the art world, therefore, than simply the Western truth that served as a yardstick. Basquiat was one of the first African-American artists to make his mark in the world, with an innovative art of unique intellectual beauty.

All sorts of questions can be asked about beauty in the art of a segregated class. Can arrogant messages on socio-political issues be called beauty? The satisfaction of experiencing art surely varies according to the beholder's background? Is it not the case that the public judges art too much from a conventionally passive attitude? Basquiat swiftly became one of the world's greatest artists of the final quarter of the twentieth century. His political indictment in the form of painting found a hearing in the white society in which he was obliged to compete as a Black man. Basquiat had a solo exhibition on 31 October 1981 – 'The Public Address Show', his first in the United States. His gallery owner, the one who offered him her basement as a studio, quickly steered his work into the most important galleries in New York. Basquiat was a brilliant artist who made his mark on contemporary art.

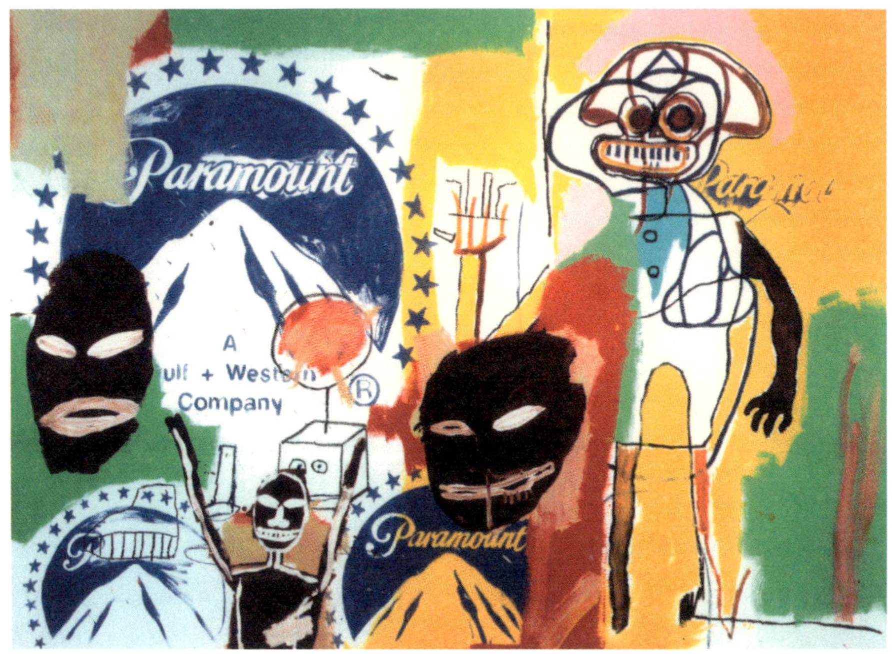

Art lovers have failed to behave sufficiently as individuals in recent decades. They form part of a social group and blend into the crowd, thoroughly permeated with a collective point of view. They tend to subordinate their preferences to the judgement of the group. Their taste in art is ready-made and is swiftly considered by the group to be the only correct one. The art market responds to this and the opinion of the group in question will make itself felt, but only locally and only for the space of one generation, which is short. New, autonomous work, by contrast, is always considered unusual. Because this art is new, it is open to criticism from the outset. Yet it is precisely for this reason that it has a greater chance of a future. It is exceedingly rare for artists who are embraced by the masses and who make a successful living through commerce also to make history. All the same, they are blindly followed by groups of people who are interested in art, who visit artists' studios, and who lap up what their guides tell them. They are all too quick to buy, without reflecting any further on the existence of the work in question. They do so out of solidarity and they choose from among the works that happen to be in the studio. Artists are well advised, however, to make a selection in advance, to ensure that they still have some say in the purchase decision. The visitor to a studio who buys on the spot before the artist has had a chance to make a preliminary selection is making a mistake. As

Andy Warhol & Jean-Michel Basquiat
Paramount, 1984
Oil paint, silkscreen ink and acrylic paint on canvas, 261.8 x 190.5 cm
Vienna, Heidi Horten Collection

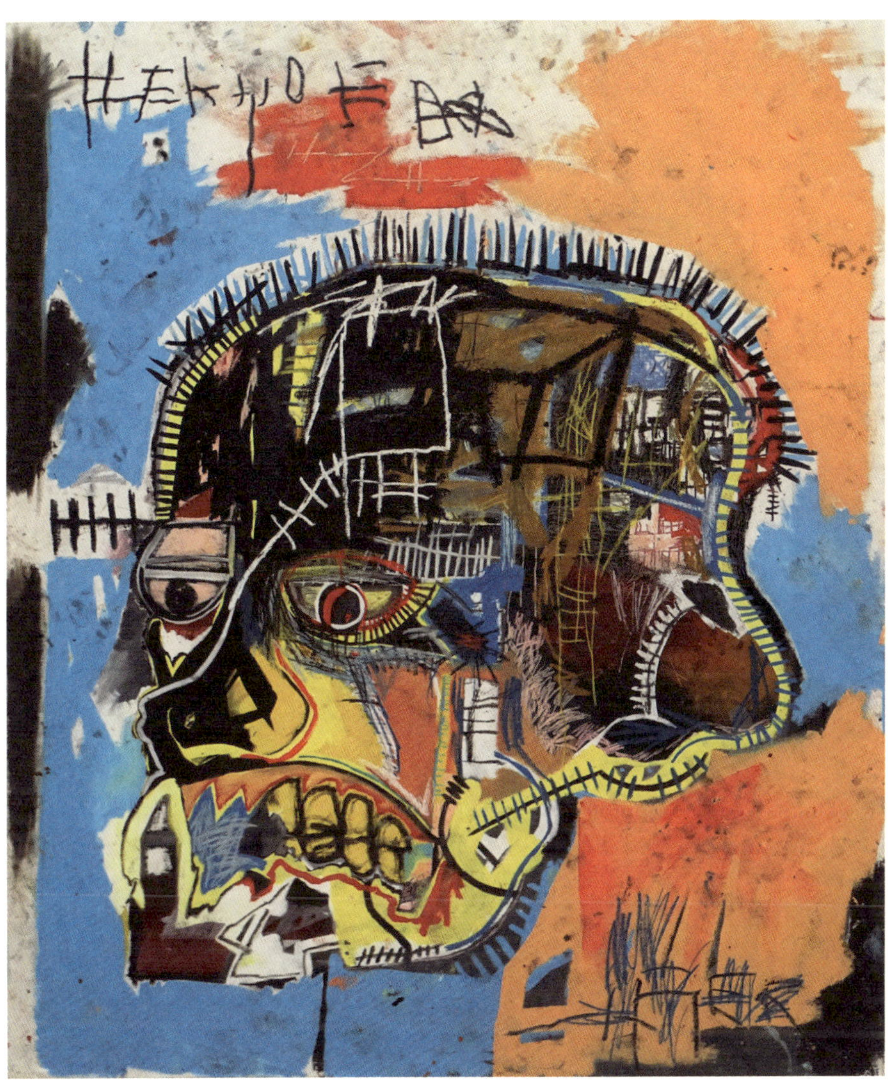

is the artist, who becomes the puppet of a uniform judgement and of the practice of collecting direct from the studio. The purchase is made under the pressure of a short-lived adrenaline rush. Buying art from artists who are ahead of their time ought not to be done under commercial pressure, shaped by current taste or admiration. A purchase based on reason and on an understanding that the work has yet to be recognized should ignore the momentary judgement of beauty, and should at the very least be visionary and define the art-historical lines of tomorrow. Buying art requires a shift in the mental and financial pain threshold: a shift that turns art criticism into a value judgement. It also requires a special effort on the collector/

Jean-Michel Basquiat
Untitled, 1981
Acrylic paint and oilstick on canvas, 205.7 × 175.9 cm
Los Angeles, The Broad

buyer's part to open themselves up to something they would never previously have chosen or paid for. Their inner visionary will make a historical judgement and approach the new standard of beauty.

It is worth asking at this point why it is that thirty thousand people a day come to gape at the *Mona Lisa* in the Louvre. Most of these visitors have seemingly fallen prey to irrationality, as they stare at the woman with the loveliest smile. Cultural tourists are chiefly motivated by the urge to pay homage to the museum and to demonstrate that they have been there. Or is it the presence of the *Mona Lisa* that has made the Louvre such an aesthetic and artistic point of reference? A visit to Leonardo's most famous work has steadily taken on the aura of a pilgrimage. The idealization of Mona Lisa's smile and the eyes that follow each visitor around threatens to reduce an entire museum to a fairground attraction.

Leonardo da Vinci painted the work around 1506. Everyone concurred that he knew how to paint a perfect facial expression and so it was that he created the most famous icon in art. No one will ever equal him in this regard. And yet the mass hysteria over one woman's smile raises all sorts of questions. Lisa's gaze and imperturbable smile are reminiscent of ancient Greek statues. The stoicism of her expression does not immediately convey a sense of happiness. Lisa Gherardini, the subject of the painting, is said to have been dissatisfied with her portrait, prompting all manner of speculation in the centuries that followed. Some have claimed that she looks mannish and that her furtive smile is that of a transvestite.

But is Mona Lisa's beauty still widely acknowledged today? Is she still considered the epitome of perfection in the twenty-first century? Some 456 years after Leonardo created his masterpiece, Andy Warhol made a portrait of Marilyn Monroe, with which he presented his own, new vision of beauty. Monroe was the sex symbol of the fifties and sixties. The actor killed herself in 1962 and was reincarnated that same year in a portrait by Warhol. She was the iconic beauty of the new era, in which she seems far more seductive than Mona Lisa: the thousands who turn out every day to gaze at Leonardo's painting do so more out of some collective hysteria than admiration for Lisa's perfect smile. Andy Warhol also succeeded brilliantly in getting enormous numbers of people to look at his work – a vast crowd who had previously shown no interest in art. He replaced Mona Lisa with Marilyn. A timid artist, who preferred to hide behind a wig and to shut himself off like an elusive frightened bird was simultaneously very much present. Warhol grabbed the attention by presenting images from among our everyday consumer purchases – from Campbell's tomato soup to Coca-Cola, and from stylish cars to beautiful women and movie stars. And by repeating them, over and over again. Warhol was gay and art historians think that Leonardo might well have been too. Yet both managed to portray the perfect

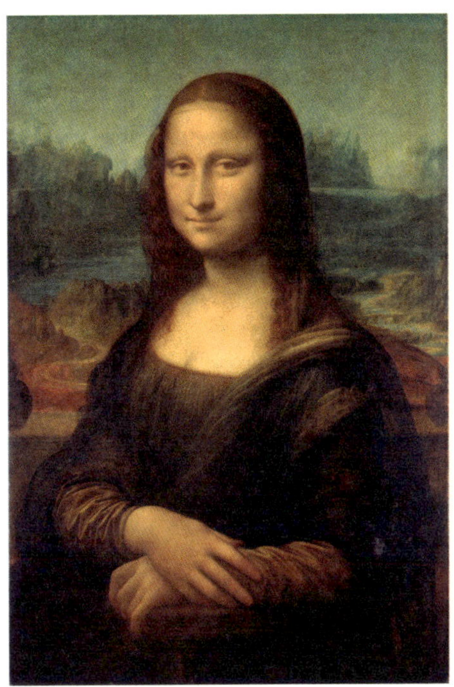

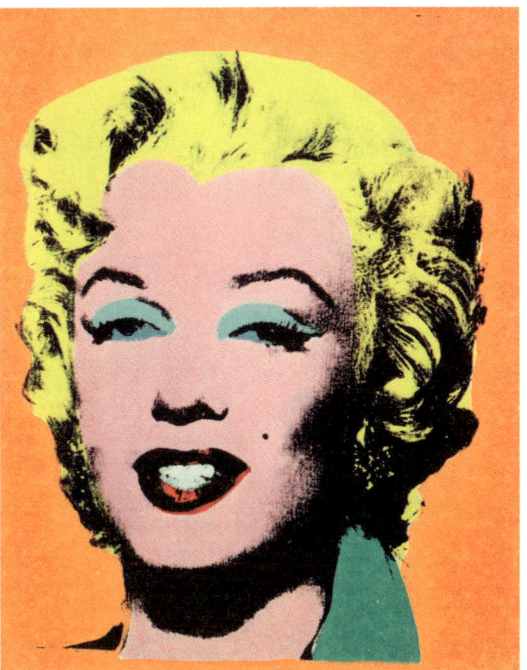

woman of their time. Warhol transformed the warm tones of Lisa's seductive beauty into cool colour fields. Marilyn Monroe's portrait, meanwhile, looked as though it was plastered in garishly coloured cosmetics and was recognized as a contemporary image. She symbolized the beauty inherent to the free American culture of the 1960s – what became the 'flower power' era. On 9 May 2022, her iconic 1964 portrait, the *Shot Sage Blue Marilyn* silkscreen on canvas measuring 101.6 x 101.6 cm, sold for $195 million at Christie's auctioneers in New York. It is one of the four 'Shot Marilyns', pierced by the bullet with which Dorothy Podber threatened Warhol at the Factory. The sale broke Pablo Picasso's record (*Les femmes d'Alger*, 1955) and the American portrait became the most expensive artwork of the twentieth century.

Great artists formulate their thoughts and create work from within. Art lovers see the result, what it is that can be viewed from the outside. For this very reason, it can be hard at times to follow the explanation offered by artists themselves concerning the growth of their work. Those who create their art from the soul and hence from within are sometimes surprised by the result they see from the outside. It is no easy matter, therefore, to deem a work of art to have succeeded based on an overarching logic. It is an extraordinary thing when a single artist on our planet of

Leonardo da Vinci
Mona Lisa, c. 1506
Oil on panel, 77 × 53 cm
Paris, Musée du Louvre

Andy Warhol
Peach Marilyn, 1962
Acrylic paint and silkscreen ink on canvas, 50.6 × 40.8 cm
Private collection

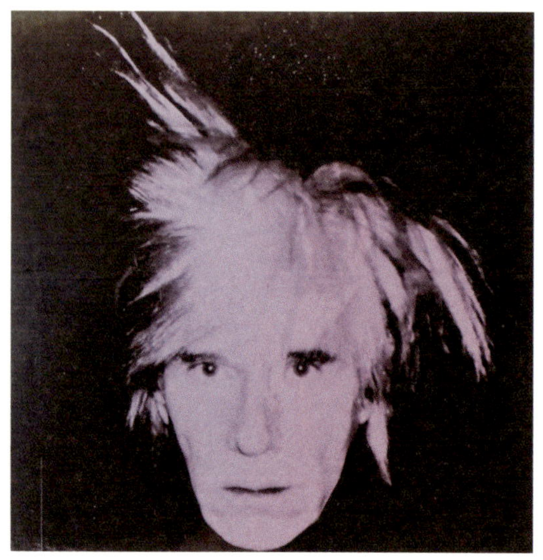

almost eight billion people can make an absolute difference. What they do, these visual artists like El Greco, Goya, Picasso, Bacon or Warhol, as well as singers, composers, philosophers and so on, can be called miraculous. Yet the most hideous dictators also operate from their inner being. In the history of art, it has always been the solitary figure with an individualized ideology who has succeeded in changing the world, never a group with a shared way of thinking. Which is why true artists can never be discovered when they seek the protection of others. And no one can track down these exceptional individuals without entering a direct dialogue with something hitherto alien to them.

In every era, the geniuses who would go on to be recognized as major artists bared their souls, leaving them extremely vulnerable. They alone understood the renewal in their artistic achievement. They posited a new beginning, to which they added nothing from the past, never thinking like a scientist, but acting in an entirely innovative manner. Geniuses detach themselves from any existing object and always proceed unpredictably. The confrontations triggered by their work fuel debate and they create a new life. These are the artists who derail society yet simultaneously recharge our thinking. Paradoxically, it is precisely through their beginning that they bring their own derailment back on track. So it is that their new creations teach us to see that art does not equate to the objects of least resistance, but rather the opposite.

Marcel Broodthaers (1924–1976) was a penniless Brussels poet and conceptual artist. Active in the 1960s, he was the key figure of the Arte povera movement. Broodthaers possessed the gift of the word and a love of the book. His work consisted of valueless materials, through which he critiqued the cultural mores of his time and in so doing interrogated the relationship between art and life. The art he created obliged viewers to judge it objectively and his work was widely criticized. It consisted of poetic irony and triggered a process of incubation in those who were curious about it. Conceptual works incorporating mussels, eggs and coal were impossible to ignore. Broodthaers did not create a neatly ordered puzzle from a jumble of parts and there is no point in searching for a narrative in it, as the power and the quality are situated in the concrete nature of his art and can be sensed immediately. Appointing

Andy Warhol
Self-Portrait, 1986
Acrylic paint and silkscreen ink on canvas, 203.5 × 203.5 cm
San Francisco Museum of Modern Art

himself director of his own imaginary museum, he filled an exhibition space with empty transport crates and plates with the names of world-renowned artists who set visitors salivating. He made artworks out of books dipped in plaster; bicycle pumps; cooking pots with empty mussel shells; panels and canvases with empty eggshells, confusing poems or nothing but his initials; and empty jam jars filled with prints of sensual lips like those of Marilyn Monroe. As a critical spokesperson for a triumphant post-modernity, Broodthaers is alluding here conceptually to the 'American smile'. Yet it is hidden and multiplied behind the glass walls of the jar, at once unattainable and a symbol of emptiness. With his jam jars bathed in sultry eroticism, the artist fed the hunger for art. His entire oeuvre is a single great artistic discourse. Marcel Broodthaers was a cultural icon who moved the art lover. He created a void in art and in doing so broadened the dialogue on its validity.

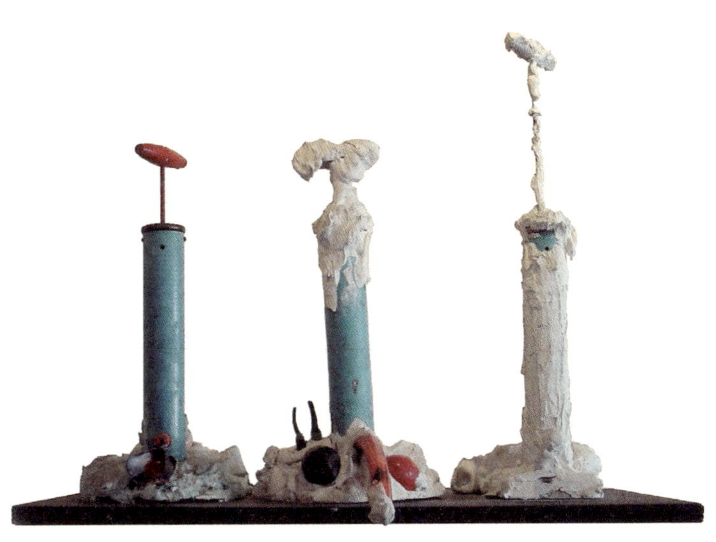

Marcel Broodthaers
Les Ancêtres, 1964
Mixed media, 55.5 × 67 × 42.5 cm
International Modern Art Foundation Belgium

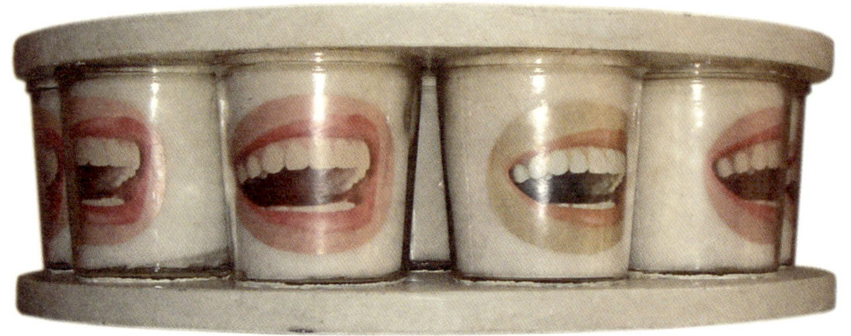

WHAT IS ART?

Can we answer the question 'what is a work of art'? It is an object with the aspects of a quasi-subject, the existence of which has great importance. Art takes no account of the viewer's judgement and seeks out boundaries in order to push them back. Art is autonomous, now as in the past, contrary to what was expected of it. There is no objective truth about a work of art and a definition of the word 'art' does not exist. Art cannot be defined in a way that is empirical or applicable to everyone's opinion. What is unknown and new in art is rarely loved and is hence also swiftly denigrated. And yet it is also thanks to the overly critical general public that this art had the opportunity to exist. Had it been accepted from the outset, it would never have been studied so thoroughly and would not have received such special attention. Innovative works of art are relevant precisely because they fall outside our expectations. Because art is nourished by constantly renewed, previously unknown ingredients, with the result that it remains an important strand of philosophy.

We humans are part of one great living story within the evolution of the universe and the Earth, because of which we are all intimately connected to everything and everyone around us. Human beings are formed by the environment in which they are raised and the circumstances in which they live. We are part of a collective culture, which entails a danger that art will focus on the lowest common denominator. Popular art destined for the masses is immune to criticism, and art is

Marcel Broodthaers
Les Bocaux (Jar-Lips), 1965
Mixed media, 40.6 × 12.5 cm
International Modern Art Foundation Belgium

done an injustice when it is commercially motivated and produced solely for the viewer's pleasure. This applies even more to contemporary art, which requires an intellectual effort rather than pandering.

If we compare the output of early avant-gardists with the abundance of art today, the professionalization of art has become problematic as it risks shifting the focus away from the artist's true métier. All the same, it is only those independent artists who follow their own path that have added to the history of the world's art. Autonomous artists have taught us how to think freely, adding value to our search for innovation. Does this mean that there is no more to today's artwork than the management of pre-digested *generation art* that panders to our desire? The commercialization of that desire has poisoned the entire world of art and constructed an art trade totally at odds with what the art world wanted. The result is a vacuum. Innovative artists ought to be approached through our capacity to think, yet this barely seems to matter any more.

Art is an existential prerequisite for our spiritual well-being, a means of communication that links viewer with maker and with many other similarly minded makers. When art connects people with the past and with the present, it becomes a vitally important means of communication. A point around which seekers like us can once again unite. While society has been critical of contemporary art, it has never set out to destroy it. Art is and remains a statement that is in society's interest. It simply takes a little thinking to accept it.

AMOR VACUI: LOVE OF EMPTINESS

The unlimited supply of art for the masses had become problematic long before the beginning of the twentieth century. Although there were scholarly studies of art, such was the influence of group inertia that the effort required to understand art that was ahead of its time proved no longer possible. The art trade capitalized on this without further thought. Those, on the other hand, who were convinced that authenticity in art leads to greatness, knew that all this could not be allowed to put a brake on development and so preferred to immerse themselves in a higher stage of thinking. True art lovers are those who make the effort to understand what artists have developed and support the ones who are brave enough to join them in thinking about it. Real art is situated in the mystery that liberates us from the organized constraints on our existence. It evades the manipulation of a systematic and partially taught view and makes life complete. Art incites people to intellectual self-edification.

There is a constant struggle between spirit and matter, and in art the fact prevails above all that spirit conquers matter! It is not matter, colour or format that build tension in a painting, nor do the material elements complete that painting. Far from it: an artwork in which the paint is more important than the intellect of the person wielding it can never be the result of positive artistic exploration. The evolution of artists tends to make them forget paint. Instead, modern painters seek the essence itself so as to overcome matter. This is a sacred definition that applies to all the arts. When conviction born of the spirit prevails over the factual, you have risen above life and attained the *amor vacui* that sweeps the *horror vacui* from its path. There is more, in other words, than seeing paint and form. Because of this, viewing a work of art is an onerous task. Learning to look at art is to walk a mental path that is turned in on itself, a delicate experiencing of the magic by which the spirit of art transcends its form. Anyone who has found this key to seeing better ought to cherish it. The sight of art is enchanting and can even help to heal us from the desperation of the times in which we live. When art is turned into a commercial event and the evolution of time ignored, the new form will be incomprehensible.

Hans Fohan
Amor Vacui G26-07, 2007
Oil on canvas, 110 × 75 cm
International Modern Art Foundation Belgium

Only a trailblazing quest that ignores the attention given to overabundant matter will break new ground despite the contemporary chaos.

The contemporary artist Hans Fohan (b. 1958) orders his thoughts and creates a space for the mystery of the void. Through his simplicity, he not only approaches the essence of art, he also offers the scope in which to address the issues within it. His work has been reduced to a kernel that says more than the fruit itself, which is merely a cloak around it. The artist's restrained enthusiasm alerts us to the discrepancy between visual reality and sensitive moral ideas, in this instance as a token of progress. What is less prominently present triggers unease and demands attention to space – space for others and space for oneself. Fohan makes visible what transcends our imaginative capacity and entices the viewer, without conspicuous or superfluous expressions. His work calls for dialogue and it probes like a creature with feelers surrounded by the human species. Fohan's oil canvases precede philosophy and point us towards Minerva's owl, a bird that only flies out when darkness falls and that teaches us how we will only become gradually aware of the absolute in art. According to the German philosopher Georg Wilhelm Friedrich Hegel, it is precisely this absolute simplicity that will lead us to actual beauty, thereby enabling us to situate current art today. Simplicity – if correctly understood – will then afford the appropriate clarification, profound and elegant. In Hans Fohan's primordial world, it is as if philosophy itself were painting his canvas, drawing us into his new formal language, replete with unarticulated poetry. Fohan does not emulate reality, but offers us instead the spirit of the intangible, the enigmatic, the absolute presence that is simultaneously absent. His autonomous world, which utterly evades conventional 'art-seeing', is situated in a distilled magical thinking. The Belgian artist's painterly vision radically opposes the prevailing conviction of what should be painted and how. He does not opt for thoughtless action, but embraces the void. His biomorphic abstraction opens up an energetic infinity, while his intercontextual role raises the visual to a higher power. Fohan's existentialist philosophy, embedded in a socio-historical context, transforms the reality in which we live today and in doing so intrigues the viewer. His biomorphic expressions might embrace the void, yet at the same time they refer to the subdued explosions of the stain that stubbornly intrigues but does not have a conventional entitlement to direct affection. The stain, the rarely avoided dialogue, represents the growth and decline of an era. His *amor vacui* stands for the silent call that demands space for the absolute right to exist.

The artist's word is pure, but usually has a long way to travel. Artists observe the world they live in, sacrifice themselves in the name of art and confront their time. They exist within the tension between life and persistence after life and raise the anchor with an urge for cultural continuity. Their creative minds act with a heightened intensity that absorbs all possible knowledge of life. Important artists create art within a new reality that never previously existed, and so their art will legitimize itself as a new culture. Only a few will find the path that brings them into a relationship with the work of this artist, for whom they become a new centrifugal force of like-minded people who swear by the need to regard art as utterly indispensable to life. All the same, not all his words hit their target: art flirts with words and the people swear against them.

THE MATING DANCE BETWEEN MARKET AND CROWD

We don't use our parents' telescope to look to the future, including the future of art. We face a necessary intervention to rein in art's degeneration: it will be needed to get the notion of art back on track. A carefully thought-out philosophy is no longer possible with such a legion of artists: a surplus of creations elevated to the status of art will continue to smoulder for centuries to come. Only if we vigorously constrain this chaos via thoughtful criticism with an eye to the next generation can we ease the burden on our artistic future a little. There is a need for someone capable of instilling in art lovers a shared sense of what is expected of art, since the conflict with prevailing and purely commercial conceptions calls for new artistic values to be established. The art market needs to reacquaint itself with the history of art and with the notion of history as such. The difference between the questions 'what is art?' and 'is this art?' urgently needs to be examined. Nobody benefits from a mass commercialization that undermines the art world and is rejected by art critics. The art world does not need a trade like this and contemporary art that is subservient to the dominance of a select club has no value either. Art isn't the property of a few individuals, whose gatherings have, incidentally, caused many a member of the club to lose their faith in art.

Our world today has a great many new resources. Digital evolution, the power of a growing free mass of people, time and money. The pressure exerted by the commercialization of art is immense, but it creates a false picture. Quantitative sales are not the same thing as true artistic value. Determining the concept of beauty on that basis – a vital part of our existence – does not benefit the art world. Sadly, the arrogance of e-commerce has the upper hand right now, but this is limiting the spontaneity of the art trade. The sale of art via a PC dehumanizes that art. The word of the gallery owner used to precede that of the critics, and now it is the computer that offers buyers new possibilities. So who is left to stimulate the work of the artists themselves? Will art still have a spontaneous future when galleries, press and patrons disappear because of the stubbornness of all those who want to stifle any artistic dialogue? Where is the shy and sincere artist to go now, when complacent internet users have neither an ear nor an eye for the spontaneous development of art itself? Does anyone today still look forward to the further evolution of tomorrow's art history?

Successful artists have a sovereign universe of their own, with its own laws and rules. Their indispensable freedom leads to a life full of desire and seeks nobody's permission. They want their voices to be heard, to have an influence on society, their art demands space and seeks out provocation. The crowd protests, but at the same time its shared anathema helps define the new thinking behind the artist's work. Nobody is excluding real life – be it past or present. Society will not limit the power of the artist, and it is precisely the avant-garde who will lead art to a new beginning. A worldwide army of art practitioners is guilty of an unlimited artisanal entertainment that has been professionalized into an industry that sells its wares in the manner of the porn business. A boundlessly consuming mass chooses its beauty all too easily with the sales system as implacable ruler. It is a situation that effectively gags art critics. When populism dehumanizes artistic perception in this way and society begins to develop a towering dung-heap of taste, the notion of 'art as communication' loses attention and the intellect loses its words. Over the past few decades, we have driven out our accumulated knowledge and the world of art has lost its universality. Our vision of art no longer exists and we are going entirely wrong. We have lost the capacity to judge art. We now value art solely in terms of its financial value and organize our spiritual architecture differently. Our environment contains a mass of information, yet we seem unable to process it. Today's art world embraces a network of many people exchanging commercial representations. Big numbers influence us and we barely realize what we are doing any more. We need to become aware of our limitations, to remain critical and act accordingly. We must retrain ourselves in how to look at art, so there is no chance of an epidemic curtailment of our artistic evolution.

A new urge to sell has clearly been apparent since the turn of the millennium and has already and disastrously taken the upper hand on occasion. Any worthwhile

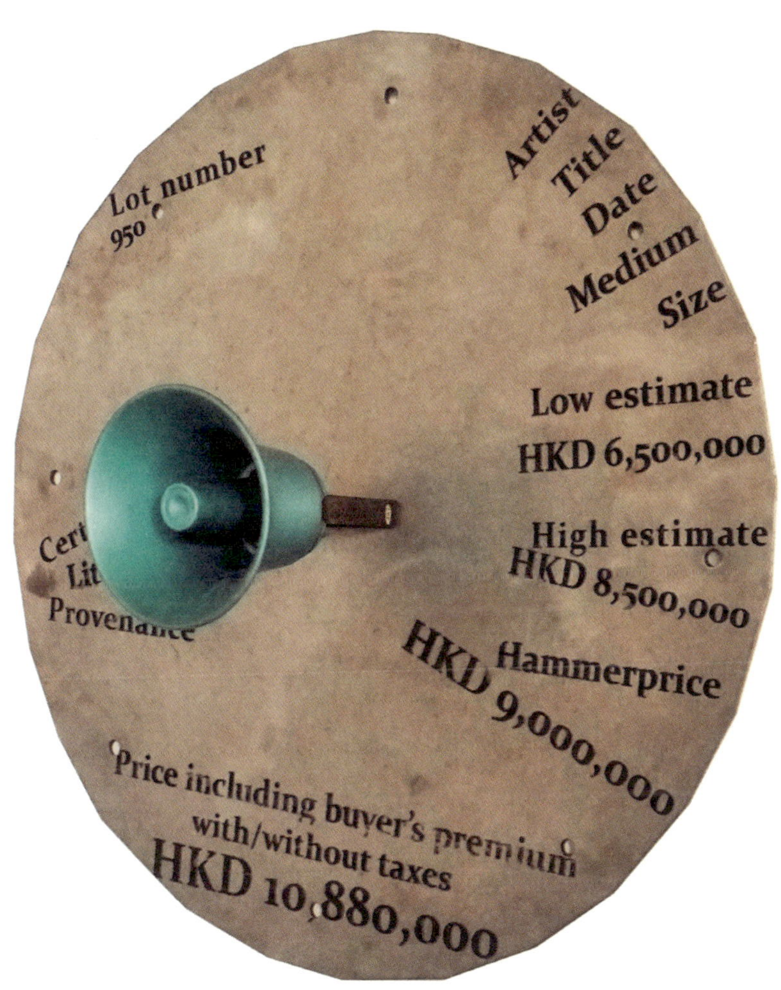

John Doe
Lot Number 950, 2017
Mixed media and oil paint on canvas, 87 × 29 cm
International Modern Art Foundation Belgium

dialogue on art disappears. Passionate gallery owners have turned out to be surplus to requirements, while patrons have seen their artists go off the rails. Auction houses have mushroomed and are disinclined to take the slightest risk. A ruthless commercialism has demoralized the art world and we have come to view art as a mass commodity. Sellers, as the new principal actor, blow wind into their own sails with exaggerated sale prices, and buyers quantify the seller's variety of tastes. The contemporary art mill grinds out a mass supply with the highest possible sales figure as ultimate motivation. The continuity of 'true timeless art' is stagnating. Art as the crowning glory of our culture is leading to drama. There is an urgent need to distance ourselves from everything that 'seems'. Art is being mistreated and intellectual interpretation is losing ground. The headstrong gallery owner has acted and traded like a murderous fascist from the very beginning. There is a real need for greater understanding of the new beginning of our twenty-first century. 'Winner-takes-all' is the new formula and is spreading fast. It fuels the global potential for imposing a culture of unlimited stupidity via the internet. Modern humanity concurs with the phenomenon of the winner, and all the things it was once able to decide on its own initiative, it now views as a risk. Because of their busy lives, people mindlessly follow the masses around them, doing what others do, so that the winner logic does it again. Auction houses are grateful to social media and to the internet in general. They play their audience between the 'low and high estimates'. Blinded by what is 'approved' of and influenced by the guide price, buyers believe they are purchasing safely. Millions of internet users see big numbers, persuading them that the work of art is interesting and the crowd admires what has been sanctified by the dominant temple of art. The artistic statement represents a disproportionate hit.

Contemporary art today runs the risk of never again being supported in its renewal, from its earliest creation onwards. Our self-reformed society, with its focus on the big numbers, manipulated or otherwise, denies art the right to dialogue and results in the creation of an impoverished culture. The bidding at an auction will never endorse or negate an artwork's historical added value. The actual value of a timeless work of art cannot be determined from a single economic perspective.

Intellectually innovative art requires research, time and protection, which makes patrons important. They defend the artistic message with a carefully thought-out vision and then bolster it. An artwork that does not perform strongly at auction puts doubt in the contemporary collector's mind. So, high sales figures are encouraged in many ways, because mediocre hacks are only too happy to fill their newspapers with them. But the bidding is manipulated in all sorts of ways, which means the low and high estimate interferes with the desire for an encounter with true art. The new culture obliges dealers to 'look' with their ears, while art critics fall into an unnatural silence. The few with an eye for the new beginning are pushed out by the new, blind collectors, who mindlessly quantify their art purchases in accordance with the most lucrative preconceived notions, while the real art world cedes its leadership and takes on a strange and unnatural new identity. In this way, the identity of art is gradually disarmed, whereas what is needed is precisely more self-manifestation. A principle is needed to tune the strings and point in the right direction. Contemporary art is not an object that can be filed away with a paperclip by any single authority. Art is a subject that must keep making itself heard as a necessary cry in the midst of society. Great art is the result of a creation born of undisturbed freedom. Old, mouldering rules on how themes ought to be visualized and the compositions that flowed from them have long since been buried. The sieve of art history has long since sifted a whole lot of creative people away, even though the wrongness of judging and condemning based on previously known standards was already realized. A great artist always has immense courage and perseverance and is the epitome of the person who cannot be bribed. Taste is not an artistic value, it is precisely the personality of its creator that satisfies the artistic conscience. Anyone who believes, on the other hand, that the financial value of art can be calculated simply by reference to a database of previous sales made on the basis of taste, is branding an artwork as an object that can be defined in advance. Contemporary art is very much not predictable and in no way an exact science. Those with an eye solely for a list full of numbers are suffering from a mental short-circuit and are no longer capable of enjoying contemporary art.

We shape our intellect through the environment in which we grow up and so we have think even more combatively. From the earliest avant-garde to the present, it has always been an absolute requirement to protect the free spirit within the art world. We have an ongoing need for a critical attitude towards art. To prefer pseudo-art is to have no sense of quality and to act as an unfree person, who condemns the creation of those who are free. Because of this, important artists have rarely been appreciated during their lifetime.

To admire art that has also been made for a generation yet to be born is, at the same time, the necessary opening for any form of progress. Free artists therefore place themselves implacably above their society's self-limited taste for beauty. The value of an artwork based on earlier sales is different from its absolute value. The low and high estimate is not a value, but a predetermined price push by self-proclaimed experts. Auction houses estimate the value of an artwork based on their turnover target. Yet art is incalculable and so we must keep on making our presence felt within this crushing reality.

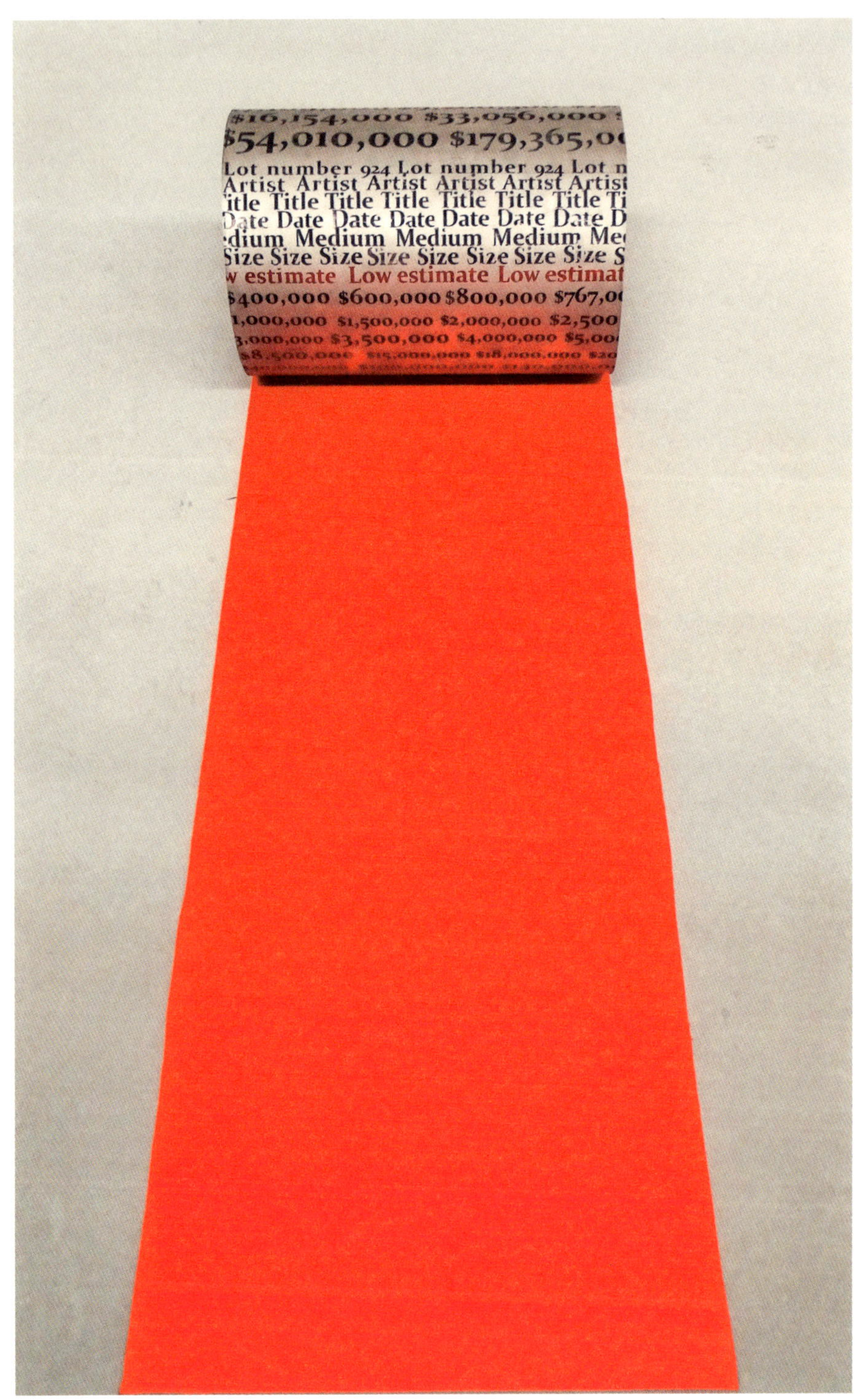

John Doe
Lot Number 924, 2017
Stainless steel, oil paint and carpet, 200 × 63 × 41 cm
International Modern Art Foundation Belgium

The art market has been flooded since the 2000s with facelifted creations that balance on the success of twentieth-century artists. The short-term performance of this work surfs on the waves of an art history that already exists. It is clear that because of this, the art world will struggle to add anything to its historical pyramid. The output of art based on polishing up what has already been achieved in the past leads only to manipulation and excess. And it is precisely this 'art-market art' that has the new generation of buyers drifting about mindlessly. There is no longer any awareness that the word 'art' arose from a historical context. This new generation of buyers does not share any art criticism and does not understand the absolute value of a patron. Art is undergoing a bewildering process of democratization, in which the desire for the necessary art world seems to have ended. The reckless determinism of the auction might be the death knell for absolute art. You have the art trade and you have the art world, and this is not the first time that the former has existed outside the latter. It means that the artist deemed most popular is not part of the art world, while another, who is much less known but who is perfecting their oeuvre with seriousness, should really be on the art world's radar. Many of the people in the art world who hold themselves up as artists are, therefore, nothing of the sort. There is a substantial difference, after all, between the temporary art trade and the definitive art world.

Within the biased culture of Western collectors, NFTs (Non-Fungible Tokens), are also available for sale nowadays. This recent invention has its adherents in the art world too, and above all in the art market. An artwork in the form of a digital object is linked to the NFT, which is a digital certificate of ownership. It is registered via blockchain, given a unique programming code and linked to the buyer's crypto wallet. The database is public and both the digital object and the transaction history, along with other information, can be viewed by anyone. NFTs are traded using crypto-currencies on various websites, but they are already being offered at auctions too – a logical development in our digital age. The key characteristic of NFTs is that they are not freely exchangeable or replaceable by another similar token. They thus certify a commitment to something digital, such as an image. Whoever purchases one obtains the certificate of authenticity and proof of ownership of the object, but entirely digitally. The token works anywhere in the world, provided you have a computer. This is entirely comparable, on the face of it, with a physical work of art accompanied by a certificate, with which the owner also proves their ownership. It is claimed that the digital aspect of NFTs offers greater transparency and excludes forgeries. The question is whether this security truly is guaranteed. Nor may there be any misunderstanding of its unique character. Much of this digital art is distributed in large editions, each of which has a unique code. No different, in that respect, to numbered lithographs, say, in large editions.

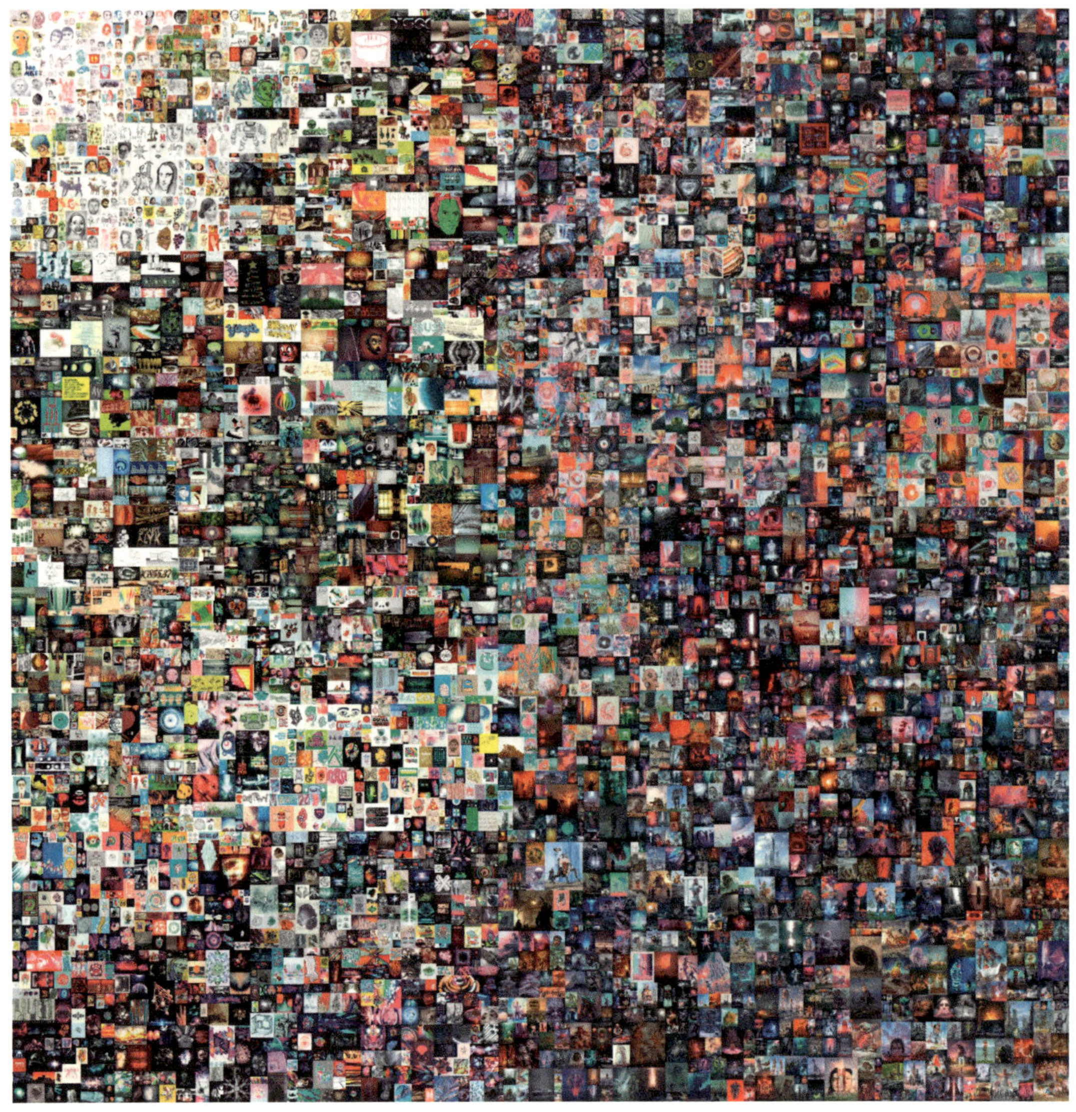

A digital work of art, kept in a virtual safe, can already command eye-watering amounts of virtual money. The new generation of creators of art like this are viewed as young artists and their buyers multiply their digital currency a hundred-fold. Technology traders are quick to pay with virtual currencies such as bitcoin or ether, and earn considerable amounts of capital, albeit in the form of digital currency. Consequently, this is where the purchase price of all things hip is moved. They view

Beeple
Everydays: The First 5000 Days, 2007–21
NFT – crypto art, 21069 × 21069 pixels

their art purchases as genuine trophies, even when they have no actual value as art. There is a gulf between these digital art amateurs and the anarchist-intellectual art lovers of the past. Whereas it was not until six years after the death of Pablo Picasso, the founder of modern art, that a painting of his first sold for over a million dollars, the monetary value of work by a young artist today is determined by the digital currency after some efficient digital marketing. Due to the digital gold rush, cryptocurrency has stripped the current market for art and collectibles of any constructive price-setting. It is hard to view this young art as the equal of its predecessor, not least because digital art frequently suffers from a loss of aesthetic value. In this regard, our century marks a break with the past. The trigger technology represented by NFTs might be the most important innovation of our time, therefore, but it is developing in terms of price a lot more than it is of artistic value. Are these online buyers pursuing their standard of beauty, or are they paying for the opportunity to make themselves famous as the owner of a particular digital object, which they might then sell on? They are chiefly interested in the digital aspect, which means that the purchased images do not yet have any real artistic value and their work of art itself does not yet have a right to exist in art history. What's more, they are fickle – everything needs to happen quickly and is short-lived. As a work of art, their 'unique' digital collector's item is the antithesis of what the art world has produced in the past, and the digital picture looks more like the result of a non-physical trading game. Are we not losing an important property of art, here, namely a tangible object?

The strength of an NFT lies in the additional protection it affords to the authenticity of the artwork traded with it, with which the intellectual property of the digital artist is secured worldwide. The coding means that digital theft of the many ideas that this generation creates in word or image can be prevented. The question then is whether a slight change to the digital object might not result in a new unique piece? The American digital artist Michael Winkelmann (1981) worked from 2007 to 2020 on his *Everydays: The First 5000 Days* – a digital collage consisting of five thousand images. The artwork consists solely of a JPEG file of 21,069 × 21,069 pixels. On 11 March 2021, Christie's auctioneers sold the digital certificate of ownership belonging to Beeple, Winkelmann's pseudonym, for $69.3m. Each of the five thousand images is also available within the digital system in multiple editions. It is precisely here that a critical approach to the word 'unique' – frequently interpreted as 'non-fungible' – is appropriate. Unlike physical art, where an original painting, say, consists of the paint and its support, a copy of the original in this instance is identical to the original itself. Digital copies digital. The NFT might currently have attained the level of a new technique in art, albeit digital, but no artist has yet emerged as innovative within that technique. So far, there is no new NFT artist to

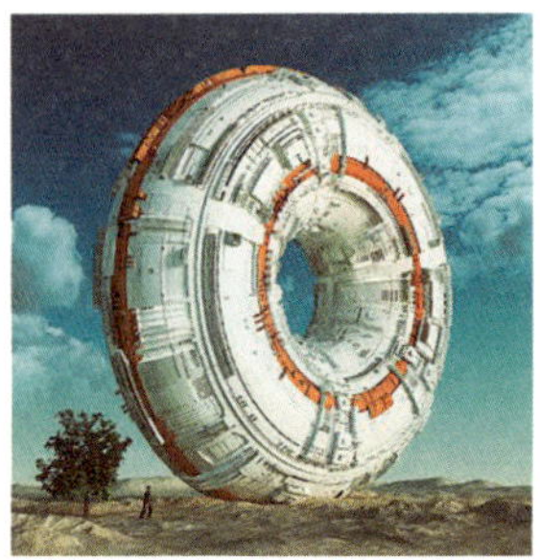

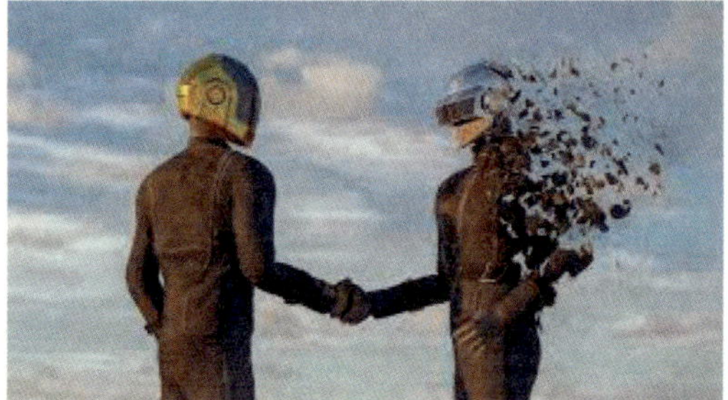

be found who has produced any work that undeniably confirms the importance of their existence. There is no difference, moreover, between original and editions. The temptation to distribute editions is quick to arise and is unavoidable, as millions of crypto speculators are there to prey on them.

Either we are witnessing the peak of a short-lived crypto art bubble, or we are at the beginning of a new chapter, in which NFT art, for example, turns into a mass aesthetic form. A great many questions still arise regarding the true value of much of the art trade in these early decades of the twenty-first century. Is true artistic value to be found in today's repertoire of auction tricks, or in the reality behind the art-historical canons to the end of the twentieth century and what might follow? Fortunately, many museum curators, critics and collectors have not allowed themselves to be distracted from the old art values.

FUCK YOURSELF ART

Fuck Yourself Art is a manifesto shown at the 2017 Venice Biennale, consisting of artworks by John Doe that analyse the function that art continues to fulfil within our contemporary social reality. His concept offers an avant-garde critique of the new zeitgeist, with canvases, installations and sculptures that resist the imposed new order, in which collectors merely participate in a bidding war of self-regulating numbers. John Doe's work anticipates the statement of the new collector, the spirit

Beeple
Everydays: One of the 5000 Works
NFT – crypto art

Beeple
Everydays: One of the 5000 Works
NFT – crypto art

of the twenty-first century. How long will this century continue to nurture such a predetermined art trade for its numbers? Surely the three key characteristics of an art collector are knowledge, courage and an eye for quality? Does the love of art continue to advance, or will this nihilism lead towards the end of our art history? What does contemporary art mean any more without a patron? Can the true artists who criticize their society still be heard by that society, in which the word 'art' has been transformed into 'cash'? Does this leave contemporary art simply as the mating of a clever market with a brainwashed mass? Have artists been left standing alongside the real stage while the art world loses its historically shaped pyramid?

Money motivates the art trade, but elicits the wrong behaviour. The auction market dissolves the art principle and its database, which has already ordered prices based on the low and high estimate, and rejects the label of art history. Modern and contemporary art objects have become investments and have created the new phenomenon of the 'art flipper'. Today's auction market is a casino, in which the mega-rich are treated with awe for buying things they don't even want to hang on their walls. The new gold silences the artist and misdirects a worldwide view of art. Art has become an investment, whether long or short term. Art flippers play the artwork, they buy and sell things for which they have no affection. They are poisoning the purpose of art. Art has become an alternative to investing in silver, gold or, more recently, bitcoin. All the same, it is still necessary to consider art that lies beyond all boundaries as relevant. Which intellect will still 'voluntarily' stand up to the titans of art capital to shed light on all the prevailing misinterpretations? Does a person who has been seduced by numbers have a greater capacity to understand art than those who have not been so manipulated, or only to a moderate extent? Will art cease to be a collective asset, as only the ultra-rich can still afford to buy an artwork? Along with a discrepancy between today's rich collector and public poverty, an unsustainable competition has arisen between museums and top international galleries, which, sadly, has made incestuous behaviour entirely logical. There is a pressing need for protective measures to avoid the end of art history.

In the space of just twenty years, between the low and high estimate, the auction world has increased the sale of modern and contemporary art by no less than 1500%. The price of work by a select group of young artists within the system has swiftly increased a hundred-fold. It seems as though 'fuck yourself' bestows a bonus point, adding a zero to the bid. Power tends to corrupt and absolute power can corrupt absolutely. Where is the means of control that will protect this mechanism from the downward spiral of arbitrariness leading to decay and corruption? Art has a function and must continue to distinguish itself in this rapidly changing society. Making a quick buck on the back of overrated mass taste harms the value of real art

Lot number
456

Artist

Title

Date

Medium

Size

Low estimate

$6,000,000

High estimate

$8,000,000

Hammerprice

$6,200,000

Price including buyer's premium with/without taxes

$7,109,000

Certificate

Literature

Provenance

John Doe
Lot Number 456, 2017
Oil on canvas, 180 × 150 cm
International Modern Art Foundation Belgium

and all its potential. Art is crying out like never before for identity and is demanding a life without stifled freedom. The artist, the dealer, the art critic, the auctioneer and the art lover all stand to lose by the intoxication of this blind ride.

Salvator Mundi or *Christ with a Crystal Sphere*, attributed to Leonardo da Vinci, was sold in November 2017 for $450.3m, making it the most expensive work of art ever. Leonardo is said to have received the commission from the French royal family, who gave the painting in 1625 to Princess Henrietta Maria. She then took it with her to England when she married the future King Charles I. It belonged in the nineteenth century to the British collector Sir Frederick Cook. Once it had passed out of royal ownership, all manner of experts ceased to ascribe the work to Leonardo. In 1958, Sotheby's – the renowned auctioneers with a tradition dating back to 1744 – declared that it had been painted by Giovanni Antonio Boltraffio (1466/67–1516), a studio assistant of Leonardo. The sale value of the painting stood at no more than £45 as a result! In 2005, half a century later, the American art dealer Alexander Parish purchased the now unimportant *Salvator Mundi* for a paltry $1,175. Seeking a second opinion to counterbalance the earlier expertise that the auction house had imposed from its position of power, the owner had the painting investigated further. Besides undergoing major restoration, it also became the object of a murky history. Having been restored, it was authenticated as a bona fide Leonardo da Vinci and was exhibited and catalogued as such at the National Gallery in London in 2011. Christ's crystal ball foretold good news. By 2013, *Christ as Salvator Mundi* was considered a masterpiece and changed hands twice in less than a year. It sold a first time for just under $80m and, twelve months later, a Russian billionaire paid $127.5m for it. Eight years before, in 2005, a true art lover who was the then owner of what would become the most expensive work of art of all time, was informed that his discovery had been painted by an *amateur d'époque*. This person who had recognized its quality received $700 in pocket change, after premiums. A little later, now attributed to Leonardo da Vinci and dated to around 1500, the painting ended up between the insidious guide rails of the auction house, the low and high estimate. The art auction system read its future in the crystal ball and brought its commercial acumen to bear. Early art can count on little attention from today's investors. The former owner watched as the Renaissance piece effectively shifted to the category of contemporary art. *Christ as Salvator Mundi* was resurrected in a different age and, thanks to some skilled lobbying, changed hands for 45,000 times the aforementioned pocket change. This raises some questions, to say the least. As the icing on the cake, *Salvator Mundi* was purchased by the Crown Prince of Saudi Arabia, whose Islamic religion prohibits the depiction of saints, prophets and so forth, yet regards Christ as a prophet. Christ's crystal ball not only forecast what is undoubtedly the most profitable deal in the

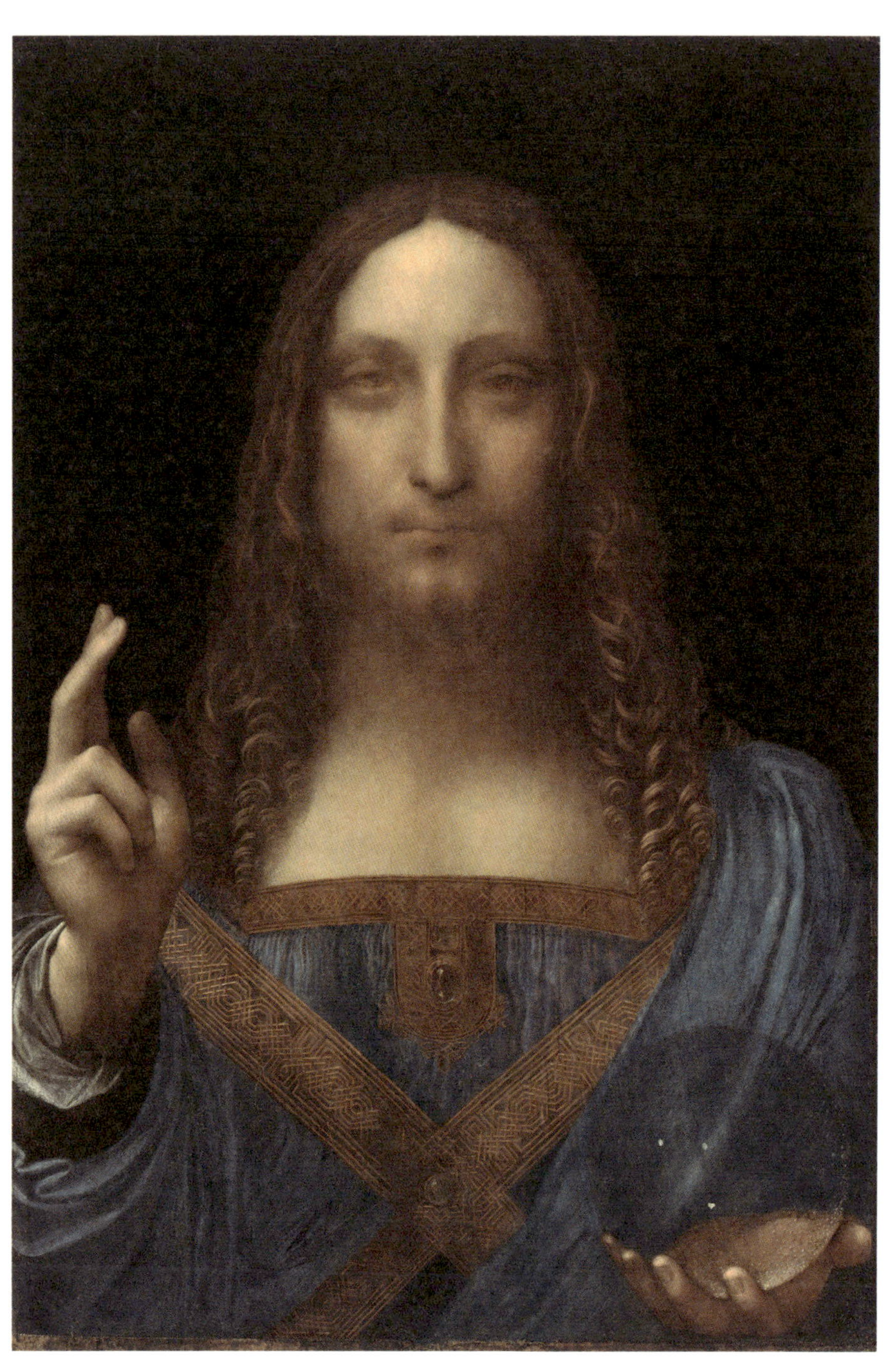

Studio of Leonardo da Vinci (?)
Salvator Mundi, c. 1505–09
Oil on panel, 65.5 × 45.1 cm
Musée du Louvre Abu Dhabi

history of the art world, it also casts a light on the peculiarities of other religious beliefs. All manner of doubts having been raised about the authenticity of the canvas, it was not included in the major Leonardo da Vinci exhibition in the Louvre at the end of 2019, even in the face of political lobbying. The work remains an object of discussion to this day between all sorts of museums, researchers and art experts. It is not even clear where it is located – not in the Abu Dhabi Louvre, at any rate, where it was due to be given pride of place. *Salvator Mundi* – possibly still no more than a studio work – remains every bit as enigmatic as the Mona Lisa's smile.

Four centuries ago, the Netherlands experienced a 'Golden Age' sustained by its naval power and numerous colonies. The region was highly developed economically and where this prosperity existed, people cast around for investments, leading in turn to the very first economic bubble: a price war that bears a lot of comparison with what has been happening in the art world of the early twenty-first century. It all began with the Dutch scientist Carolus Clusius (1526–1609), who adored tulips and created a beautiful garden for himself in Leiden. Clusius grew his tulips with great passion and successfully cultivated some exceptional blooms. He had no intention of enriching himself through his botanical skills, but others were quick to detect the commercial potential. People stole his tulips and harvested the bulbs to grow more of them. Varieties were hybridized and people fell for the splendour of these new, ornamental flowers, which were grown in ever greater numbers. The economy was thriving in this Golden Age, there was ample capital around and people were seeking around for ways to invest their money. The Dutch Republic had a capitalist economy and investors there promoted the collection of tulips as something valuable. Tulips began to be treated like gemstones. An outbreak of plague then resulted in heightened fatalities and the abrupt enrichment of the victims' younger heirs. Not a million miles away from what has been happening recently: with the world gripped by the Covid pandemic, the masses in front of their computer screens focused even more on the winner-takes-all principle. In the seventeenth century, just like today, young people invested in what was shoved in front of them. They leapt en masse into tulip bulbs, the price of which shot up. The low estimate kept climbing, with each person persuading the next of how much richer they stood to become. Investors egged each other on and bragged about their tulip bulbs. Tulip mania showed no sign of abating, but all that cloning, crossing and multiplying of the flowers left the tulips themselves vulnerable to viral infection. Their lovely colour was lost, and sick plants were no longer able to reproduce. Investors nevertheless continued to buy blindly, with the promise that a new season would bring beautiful new bulbs. Mass hysteria pushed logic aside. Three tulips were enough to buy an inn and a single bulb could be as valuable as a grand Amsterdam canalside house. Seventeenth-century citizens did not know any better and their notorious tulip mania turned out to be a bubble. Prices collapsed in February 1637, at which point it finally dawned on people that the trade in flower bulbs was a castle in the air.

THE VALUE OF EXISTENCE

If art had never existed and the world had never known its artists, it would have been economic power that prevailed over all else. Each continent might still have fought for its life, yet its existence would not have been remembered for that reason. A great work of art that marked a particular era also marks the place of its creation. Horizontal timelines thus feature 'a creation' and by extension a genesis, but a timelessness too. Art has many important aspects that allow it to be remembered. What's more, many a place has adopted a certain position because of art. They continue to attract generation after generation of visitors, who travel to the place where a famous work of art is located. Without an artistic history, past ages and certain locations would have little residual value if they had survived purely for economic motives.

The evolution of time has left us with a perceptive capacity that makes us critical of everything we accept as the new normal. We are no longer at a stage of old rules that place us with our backs to the wall. The new era teaches us to think differently, which means we are open to different opinions, we feel free and we accept the right of others to express themselves as free people. The same goes for artists, who demand even more scope in which to stimulate our free thinking. They battle against anyone who shows signs of spiritual short-circuit and do everything in their power to teach others to accept the existence of their work. They create works of art that embody an incorruptible sincerity and make themselves receptive to criticism, since without their avant-garde position there would be no criticism and we would be left looking at the end of art. They deliberately oppose the beauty of vacuous art imitation. Those who live within the rules are willing to die after a life of no resistance. Victims like this are in need, the artist believes, of a wake-up call. Neither art nor life itself has any classical aesthetic criteria. Nothing needs to be subject to artisanal standards, in which a work is judged according to its level of artistic skill and

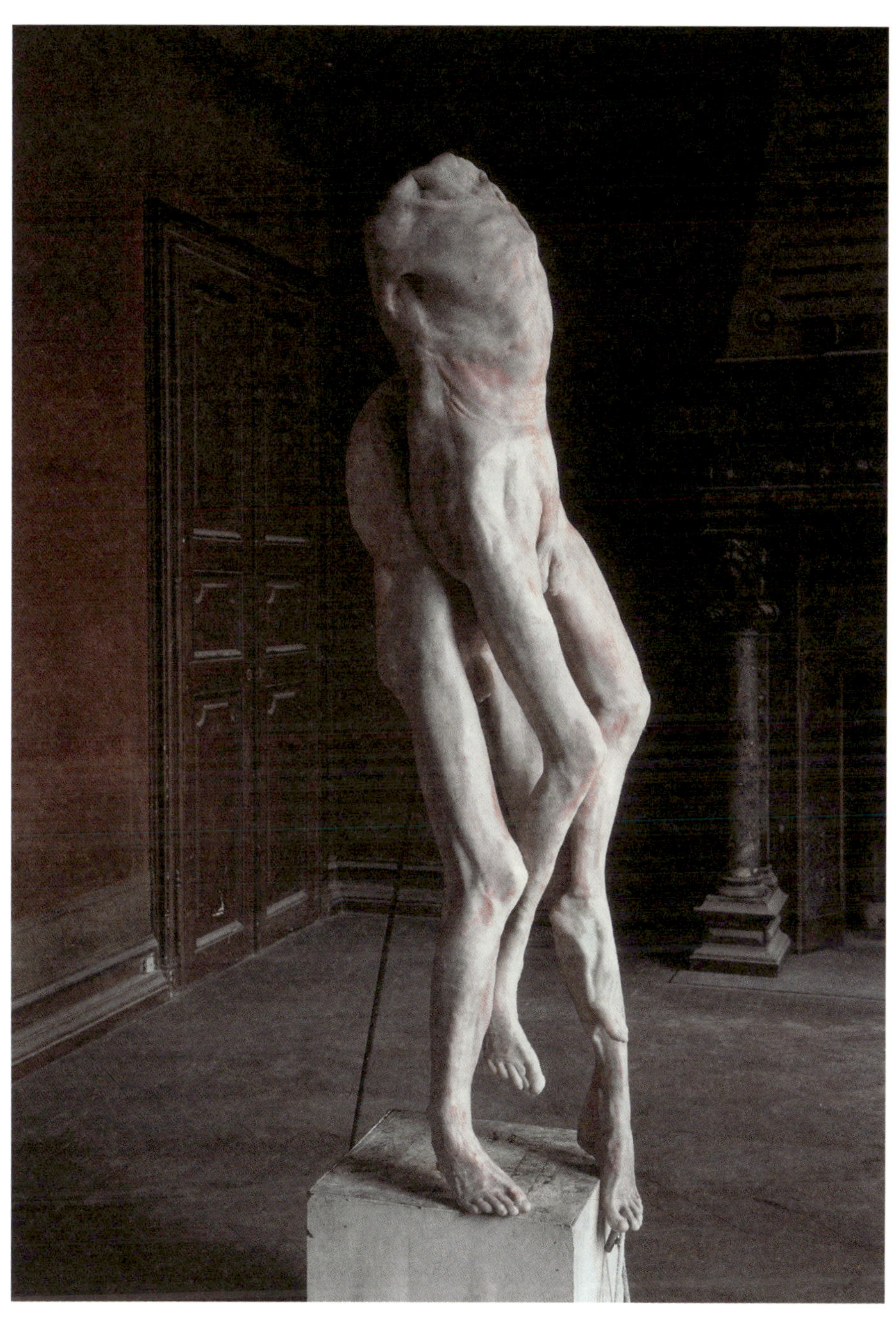

Berlinde De Bruyckere
Pietà, 2008
Wax, wood, metal and epoxy, 237 × 58 × 54 cm
Washington DC, Podesta Collection

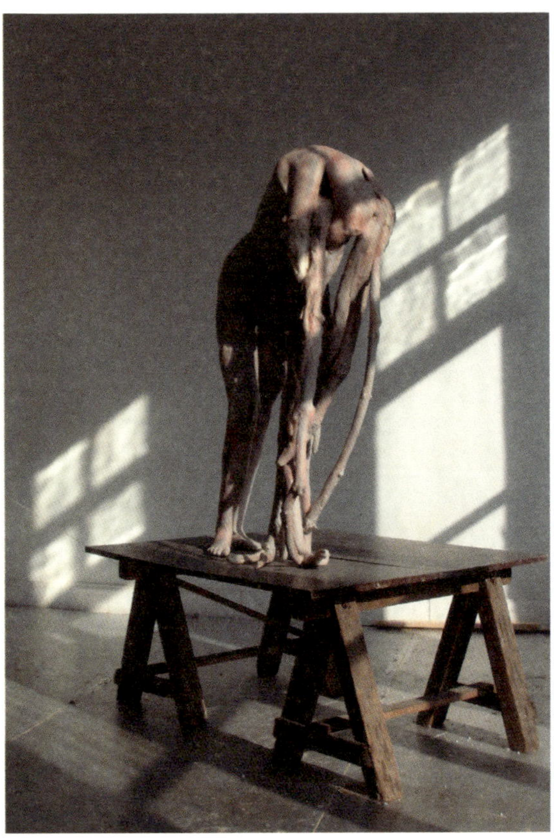

technical commitment. The artwork itself must be provocative – that is the imperative behind unregulated ideas and needs. Consequently, those who seek to judge art are obliged to measure the unmeasurable and to compare the incomparable. Art, which the essential patron has had to recuperate in its defencelessness, cannot even prove its own existence. It is the artistic act itself which – mostly at a much later date – the public will view as a quasi-subject at the beginning of the new age from which it sprang and will persist forever.

Art is indefinable since it has no quality that is all-encompassing and is frequently reduced to a psychological fact. Art might have an aesthetic aspect, but that is not its absolute purpose. The passive presence of an aesthetic component is still not a closed concept that explains why art is universal. Contemporary art has a pluralistic character that allows different cultures and interest groups to coexist and uses indefinable means to touch the soul. In the best case, therefore, art is an open concept.

Berlinde De Bruyckere
Marthe, 2008 (work in progress)
Wax, wood, metal and epoxy, 280 × 172.5 × 119.5 cm
Fondazione Sandretto Rebaudengo collection
Author's photograph taken in the artist's studio on 9 September 2008

Three hundred and fifty years after Bernini's *Ecstasy of St Theresa*, we discover the expressive nudity in the work of Berlinde De Bruyckere (b. 1964). Animal hides take the place of the centuries-old habits of the saints and embrace human suffering. There is nothing in her work to satisfy the cheery desire of those who believe that art offers absolute peace of mind. Her human bodies lack faces, avoid direct communication and thus stir the soul. The sight of her headless wax sculptures with the colour of dead skin, confuses our mental order, the intersection between life and death pressing the art lover towards the introspection and respite needed for any dialogue concerning death to be possible. Her work, born of a fascination with everything contrary to what is attractive and beautiful, offers us renewed comfort and beauty. De Bruyckere's natural yet simultaneously gruesome representations of humans and animals trigger fears of a loss of control over our own emotions, freedom and security. Human body parts, bones and limbs, testicles and labia are a metaphor that eroticizes and dramatizes, while crying out at once to be touched.

The Belgian artist's spontaneous openness enables her to create a sense of dread, just as her world, between life and death, alludes to the essence of our existence. The vulnerability of her velvety animal hides fascinates us and makes us aware of who we are and of what we are a part. De Bruyckere's carnal, physical nudity offers us the space for emotional pain, placing it in opposition to religion itself. The sacred nature of her work is not concerned with redemption in the biblical sense, but with the acceptance of everything that is part of our existence. Despite its highly erotic undertones, her mystical visual language is proof of our absolute nakedness in the face of each new beginning, in which the spectator can make out a *pietà of the psyche*.

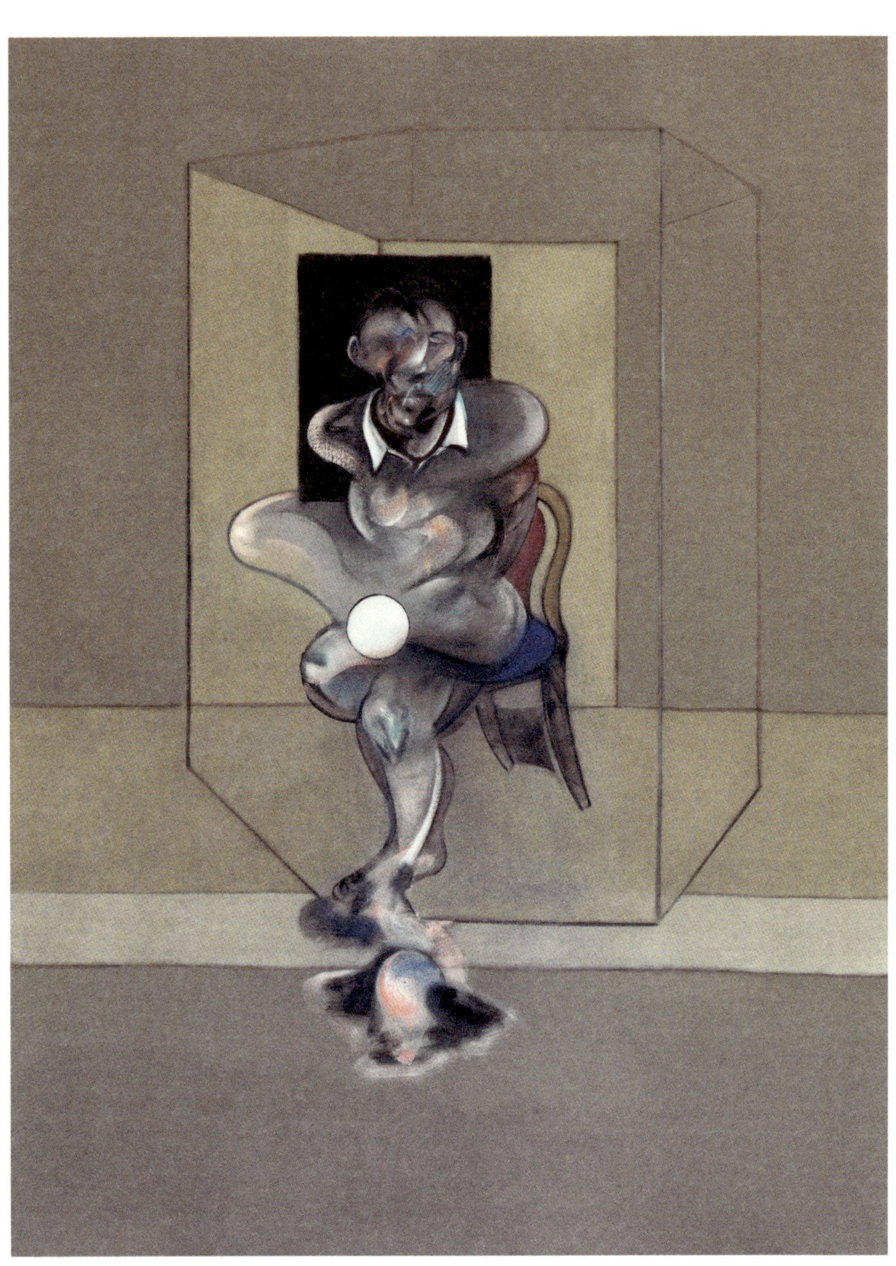

Francis Bacon
Study for Self-Portrait, 1976
Oil and pastel on canvas, 198 × 147.5 cm
Sydney, Art Gallery of New South Wales

THE FEARLESS NONCONFORMIST

Nonconformists – those who refuse to bend to prevailing norms and rules – are only acknowledged after their death, yet it is to them that modern art owes its grandeur. They possessed courage and perseverance, did not fear criticism and were themselves extremely critical. They took a close look at existing conventions and in doing so created new possibilities for art. It is safe to assume that the early works of Francis Bacon (1909–1992) were not considered beautiful at the time. The artist created from his innermost self and arrived at the most alienating paintings through a kind of necessity. His works of art are especially authentic, precisely because of the way they reflect human suffering. Anyone who saw them and looked at what could be seen in them, was moved. The Irish-born, London-based artist used a sense of drama to reach the viewer, the fact that painting was always an absolute necessity to him meaning that he outdid many other artists in this respect. Bacon painted the mirror of his soul, which will now survive forever. His oil paintings are universal in content, but real too: his work hits home because that is what his style does. Bacon's work came to be because it had to.

A painting by Francis Bacon is a vehicle for everything that hurts. He painted anything but what is beautiful. When you view his work, you must distance yourself from it psychologically, as any personal connection could trigger a sense of aversion. The dislocation of beauty renders it impossible to enjoy the beautiful reality. Bacon distorts human bodies and presents images of raw meat of a kind you only see at the butcher's. You need space – space for the mind – to view his work. Before you can experience the intrinsic value of his work, you must first overcome your repugnance. It would be wrong to reduce a work by Francis Bacon to mere plasticity, as this utterly fails to do justice to his quality. This artist is, perhaps, the best example of a quasi-subject in the approach to modern and contemporary art: he proved the importance of art by breaking through the compositional structure and going to the core of every subjective emotion.

Bacon's portraits are like dehumanized psychological monsters lacking any anecdotal value. Through his deconstructivist mode of painting, he avoided any unique or positive image of the human being. His paintings are disillusioning because his oeuvre lacks any attempt to embrace affability. It is as if Bacon were doing everything in his power to evade every human contact. There is nothing in his deconstruction of the human body that is reduced to naked beauty. He dehumanizes,

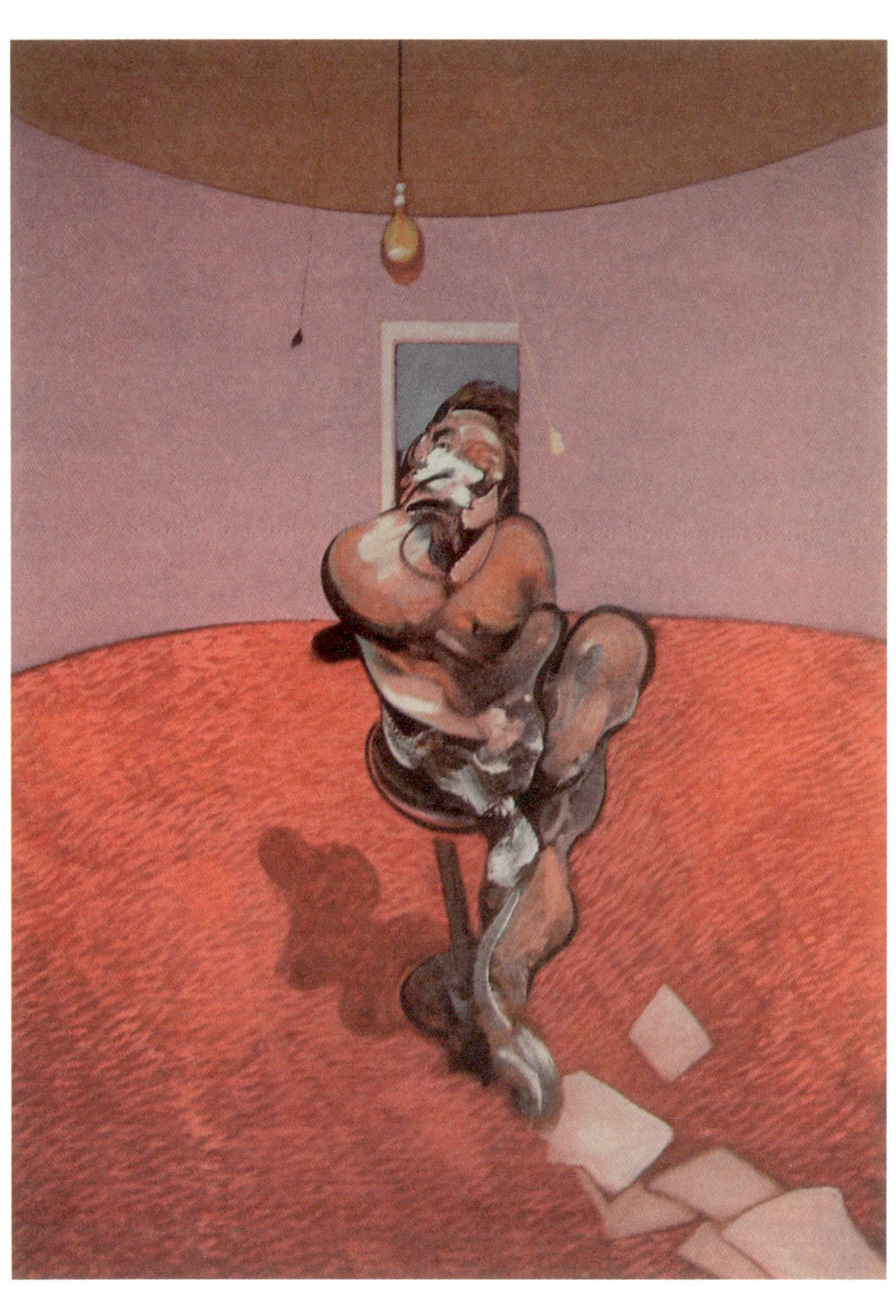

Francis Bacon
Portrait of Georges Dyer Talking, 1966
Oil on canvas, 198 × 147.5 cm
Private collection

yet retains the shape and position of the face, so that the bodies retain an element of corporeality. They are isolated figures: there is nothing in either the person or the space to allude to any contact with others. Bacon paints the misery of our world and the loneliness of the human being. He destroys all peaceful existence in the world, sanctifies bad taste and ugliness. Nothing seems beautiful any more.

All the same, with his manifesto for chaos, the painter brilliantly posits an aesthetic desire and a form of beauty: he destroys for the sake of the new beginning. Through his work, he leads the viewer out of a desolate negativity into a new world – his new world, one in which men and women are indistinguishable, a world without gender or eroticism. Bacon's work, which is anti-humanist in the extreme, also clearly stands for atheism. If human perfection in both body and mind equates to nature and nature was supposedly created by God, then humanity bends to the will of its creator. Bacon demystifies humanity and creator alike, using a negative religiosity to offer his viewers precisely the space required by the importance of his art. He paints grinning prelates and popes, destroys the human and renders invisible reality visible. Through his symbolic formal language, Bacon shows us that the purely human does not imply any harmony, contact, future or salvation. Bacon's world is much more radical than that of his predecessors. There is no place in his work for splendour or humanity. His dehumanized faces and bodies are like tumours and no one will be cheered by them. No one is offered the prospect of even the slightest heart-warming contact.

So how do we explain the fact that an artist like Francis Bacon, with his utter aversion to beauty, continues to be rated supremely highly in our modern art history? You either loathe his work or admire it, consider it degrading and humiliating or accept his dreadful reality; fear the world that Bacon depicts so horrifically or find you can live with it. Either you despise his art or you understand and accept the importance of the message it conveys.

THE PATRON

Artists are oblivious to fear and prohibitions – an attitude that is sometimes criticized. Ignoring rules elicits a reaction and ultimately transgression. It is at that fork in the road that admiration is generated and where the patron is born, who has no need to explain anything. Art lovers are moved, discover the pleasure of what is, abandon the imposed rules and distance themselves from the art with which they were

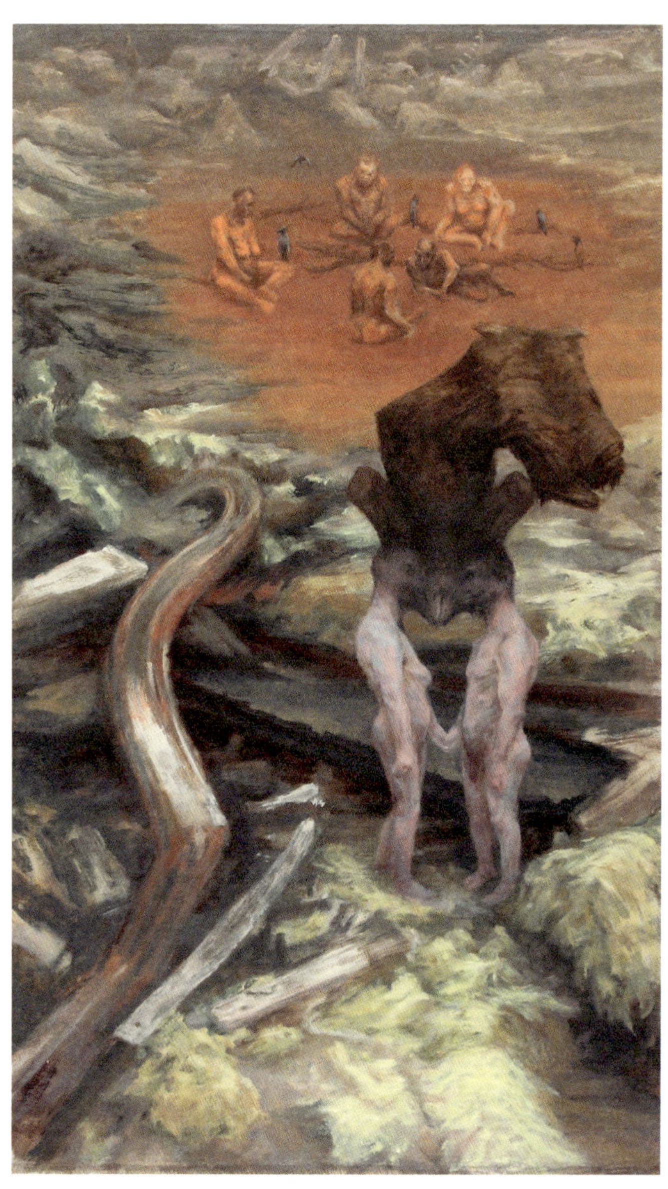

Frans Gentils
Chizofrenia, 2019
Oil on canvas, 140 × 84 cm
International Modern Art Foundation Belgium

brought up. None of that sticks, and in its place, they violate everything previously expected of art. They realize how to interact with art and embrace the higher values being offered. This love of innovative art is contagious and brings the art lover into contact with people with whom it is worthwhile discussing art as a concept. The only downside is the difficulty as a collector of biting one's tongue when faced with all the objects elevated to the status of art.

The remarkable work of Frans Gentils (b. 1951) relates to the growth of forms and the beginning of life on earth. The inscrutability and mystery of his world symbolize a reality that can never be made concrete. Gentils is an artist who brings science and humanity into symbiosis and fuses the present with the past to create a new era. He avoids any urge for beauty in his primal world. Gentils' canvases hold out a geomorphological combination of a nature recreated by human beings and a fossilized past through which time now must move on. Landscapes containing the phrenologically renewed human being are the conditional factor in his disconcerting paintings. There is nothing in his work that brings us beauty. Gentils paints people with deformed skulls, symbolizing the psyche of living in an invisible reality, a judgement of character and mental capacity. He shows us a world with a possible new way of living for humanity – a humanity waiting in perpetuity for fulfilment. His paintings and drawings confront the beholder with the past and oblige us to reflect. They are like a riddle, in which he explores the essence of our existence and brings us into contact with Darwinism.

You will never find peace with a good work of art and an uncomfortable public around you. All the same, works of art have the power to renew a person, and it is precisely this quality that allows collectors to emerge. They are constantly looking for the new methods being held out through art. There is a value in art that depends on what the work does to the viewer. It probes reality, in which there is so much to discover that one does not see. This is what is so fascinating about cultural continuity, which arises through the tension between life and persistence after life. There is a big difference in art too compared to anything that is preconditioned and denies a person the opportunity to experience a heightening of life itself. Love is always much more attractive at each new beginning waiting to be teased out. The yet-unopened book sets the heart beating faster. The concealed yearning for the unknown surely offers the absolute answer in the form of love, just as it does in art.

If art did not exist, there would be no essential need for what is unknown. And yet art has occupied a special position from the very beginning. The importance of its existence has set cultural milestones throughout the centuries. If art did not exist, human beings would have set themselves apart solely on the pretext of being free. We do not live without freedom like a paperclip. With the slightest prospect of knowledge and enough insight to keep going, we prefer to forget our old selves and to edge our way into a form of artistic self-fulfilment. The art world has had enough of a received beauty, filled with fading ideas. There is no need to cloak anything in an aesthetic mantle any more, but an unavoidable realization that universal beauty merely builds on the shards of past desire. We do not need a society in which we have to live like puppets surrounded by 'fuck yourself art' – an art whose own objects of beauty satisfy none but itself. Nobody's intellect wants to live under an 'approved' stamp.

What counts for true art is the manifestation. Today, the infinite must renew itself in the finite. This invariably imperfect manifestation stimulates the mind to impose a new standard of beauty with every unknown form – a transformation into creative art representing the unconscious infinity that is the very essence of all art. Artists touch their viewers, and if the latter perceive themselves as part of something greater, they will experience this as an ultimate emotional moment. The work of art will so overwhelm you that you too will feel the urge to see stones dance with eggs.

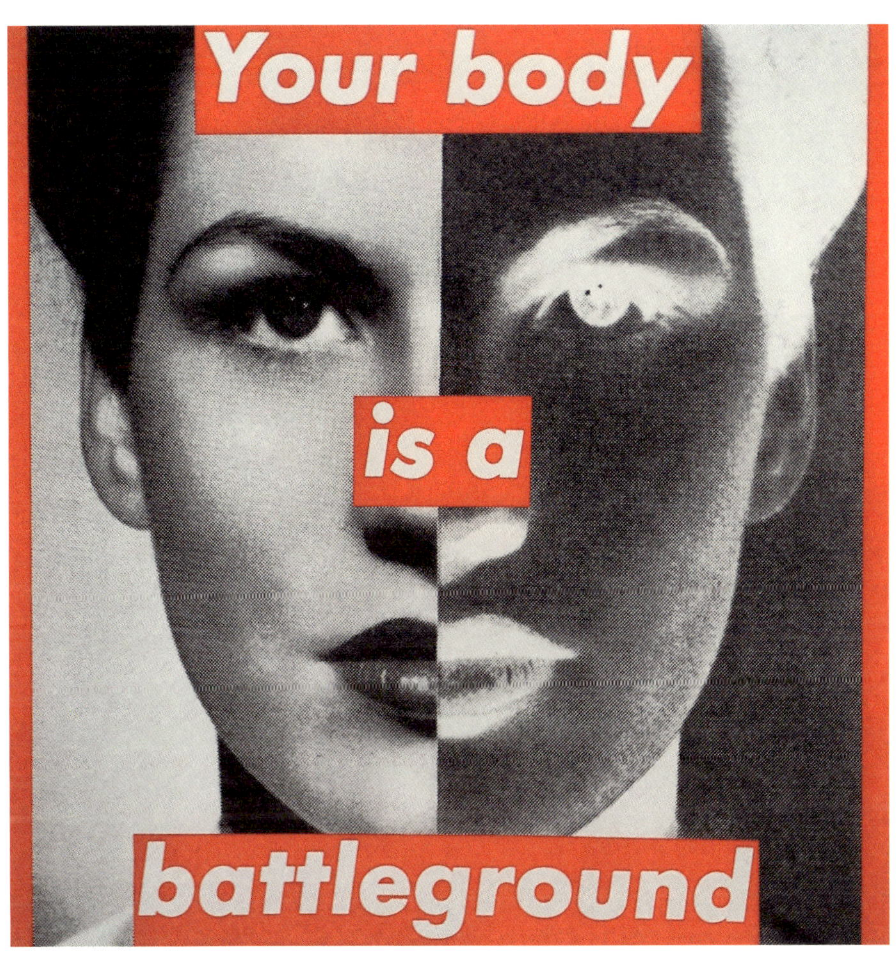

Barbara Kruger
Untitled (Your Body is a Battleground), 1989
Photographic silkscreen on vinyl, 284.5 × 284.5 cm
Los Angeles, The Broad

Photographic Credits

All images come from the archives of the International Modern Art Foundation Belgium and Ludion Publishers, with the exception of:

p. 17: Tate Images
p. 26: RMN-Grand Palais/photo RMN-GP
p. 29: Mondadori Portfolio/Electa/Arnaldo Vescovo/Bridgeman Images
p. 32: Staatliche Kunstsammlungen Dresden/Bridgeman Images
p. 44–45: Museo Nacional Centro de Arte Reina Sofía/Bridgeman Images
p. 99: Studio Berlinde de Bruyckere/photo Mirjam Devriendt

Colophon

Text
Adrian David

Translation
Ted Alkins

Graphic Design
Dylan Van Elewyck

Image Research
Marilyn Verwimp

Coordination
Ruth Ruyffelaere

Printing
Graphius

Ludion
Zennestraat 34b
1000 Brussels, Belgium
info@ludion.be
www.ludion.be

ISBN 978-94-9303-982-7
D/2022/6328/24

Cover images:
Leonardo da Vinci, *Mona Lisa*, c. 1506
Andy Warhol, *Peach Marilyn*, 1962
Keith Haring, *Heaven and Hell*, 1984
Edouard Manet, *The Execution of Emperor Maximilian*, 1868–69
Gao Brothers, *The Execution of Christ*, 2009
Marcel Broodthaers, *Les œufs de la mer*, 1966
Banksy, *Smiling Cop*, 2003

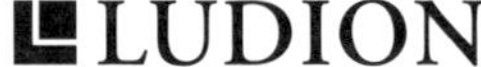